The Mac® OS X Administration Basics Cram Sheet

This Cram Sheet contains the distilled, key facts about the Mac OS X Administration Basics exam (Exam 9L0-500). Review this information before you enter the test room, paying special attention to those areas where you feel you need the most review. You can transfer any of these facts onto a blank piece of paper before beginning the exam.

OS X CORE TECHNOLOGIES

1. Darwin is the foundation of OS X; it is an Open Source community/Apple joint effort.

2. Mach 3.0 microkernel is the foundation that provides basic services for all other parts of the operating system.

3. Protected memory isolates applications in their own individual memory workspaces. In the event of an application crash, the program can be terminated without having a negative effect on other running applications or requiring a restart of the computer.

4. Advance Memory Management automatically manages physical RAM and virtual memory dynamically, as needed.

5. Virtual memory utilizes hard disk space in lieu of physical RAM.

6. Preemptive multitasking prioritizes processor tasks by order of importance.

7. Symmetric multiprocessing provides support for multiprocessor Macintosh computer systems.

8. Quartz is a powerful two-dimensional (2D) graphics-rendering system. It has built-in support for the Portable Document Form (PDF), on-the-fly rendering, compositing antialiasing. It supports multiple font form including TrueType, Postscript Type 1, and OpenType. Quartz supports Apple's Color

color-management technology, allowing for consistent and accurate color in the print/graphics environment.

9. OpenGL is an industry standard for three-dimensional (3D) graphics rendering. It provides a standard graphics Application Programming Interface (API) by which software and hardware manufacturers can build 3D applications and hardware across multiple platforms on a common standard.

10. QuickTime is Apple's cross-platform multi-media authoring and distribution engine. QuickTime is both a file format and a suite of applications.

11. Aqua is Apple's designation for Mac OS X's new graphical user interface (GUI).

12. Classic provides OS X with the ability to run a full version of Mac OS 9 in a protected memory space.

INSTALLATION

13. The minimum hardware requirements for Mac OS X include a factory-shipped G3 Macintosh CPU (~~~~~~~~~~~~~ al PowerBook G3) with ~~~~~~~~~~~~~~-supplied video card, ~~~~~~~~~~~~~~ rd disk space.

~~~~~~~~~~~~~~-system format for ~~~~~~~~ AirPort networking

and is case sensitive. In addition, UFS volumes do not show up when booted from Mac OS 9, their volume names cannot be customized, and special attention (extra effort) is needed in order to run Classic from a UFS volume.

16. The types of installations are: Single Partition, Separate Partition, and Mac OS X Only

17. The BSD Subsystem option is a required component for proper network functionality, whereas the Additional Print Drivers option installs drivers for Hewlett-Packard, Canon, and Epson printers.

FILE SYSTEM AND APPLICATION ENVIRONMENTS

18. A path is the route to a specific file, and a pathname is the map of that path.

19. Mac OS X is a true multiuser operating system.

20. Mac OS X's System folder contains critical system resources, but unlike Mac OS 9's, most users do not have access to make modifications or add more resources.

21. A Library folder contains user-customizable resources and preferences.

22. Every Mac OS X user account is provided its own home folder.

23. The ~ (tilde) represents a user's home folder within the command line.

24. The Shared folder is the place where local user accounts can share files among themselves locally on the system.

25. The Applications folder contains all user-accessible software programs.

26. Invisible items can be listed via the Go To Folder command under the Go menu in the Finder.

27. An Alias is a representative file that can dynamically locate its target file or folder, even if you move that file or folder to a different location within the same volume.

28. A symbolic link is a representative file that contains exact information (hard encoded) as to where a file or folder resides.

29. A search path is a hierarchically ordered acquisition of system resources.

30. A file extension is a designation included in the name of a file in order to help associate it with its appropriate parent application.

31. Cocoa applications are specifically developed for Mac OS X.

32. Carbon applications can run in either Mac OS 9 or OS X. When running within OS X, Carbon applications take advantage of most of OS X's modern OS features, including the Aqua interface. In order for Carbon applications to run within Mac OS 9, the CarbonLib library must be present within the Extensions folder inside the Mac OS 9 System Folder.

33. A package, sometimes referred to as a *bundle*, is a single icon point-and-click representation of an application. Just like previous Classic applications, Mac OS X's Carbon and Cocoa applications can be composed of multiple subordinate files and resources. In the GUI, all these subordinate pieces are neatly wrapped up into a representation of a single executable file for the end user.

34. Frameworks are analogous to Mac OS 9 shared libraries in that they both contain dynamically loading code that is shared by multiple applications.

35. The Mac OS X Java environment is 100-percent Java 2 Standard Edition compliant.

36. The BSD application environment usually deals with command-line executable shell scripts.

USERS AND PRIVILEGES

37. User accounts are assigned a series of attributes. These attributes include a long name, short name, password, and UID (User ID).

38. The root account, which is sometimes referred to as the *system administrator* or the *superuser account*, has complete access to all settings and files within the operating system.

39. An administrator account has enough power to get the majority of the system administration tasks done without the potential liabilities associated with the root account.

40. A normal user account does not allow system-wide administration of Mac OS X.

41. Groups are used to simplify the assignment of system access to a series of users intended to share the same level of system access.

42. Privileges (which Unix folk refer to as *permissions*) provide the control mechanism for access to files, folders, and applications within Mac OS X.

43. There are three basic types: Read, Write, Execute.

Mac® OS X Administration Basics

Samuel A. Litt

CORIOLIS

148549

Mac® OS X Administration Basics Exam Cram

The Coriolis Group, LLC
14455 N. Hayden Road
Suite 220
Scottsdale, Arizona 85260

(480)483-0192
FAX (480)483-0193
www.coriolis.com

Library of Congress Cataloging-in-Publication Data
Litt, Samuel A.
    Mac OS X administration basics : by Samuel A. Litt.
        p.   cm. -- (Exam cram)
    Includes index.
    ISBN 1-58880-234-5
    1. Electronic data processing personnel--Certification.   2. Operating systems (Computers) Certification--Study guides.   3. Mac OS.
I. Title.   II. Series.
QA76.3 .L58   2002
005.4'469--dc21

                                    2002001321
                                            CIP

Printed in the United States of America
10 9 8 7 6 5 4 3 2 1

President and CEO
Roland Elgey

Publisher
Al Valvano

Associate Publisher
Katherine R. Hartlove

Acquisitions Editor
Sharon Linsenbach

Development Editor
Deb Doorley

Product Marketing Manager
Jeff Johnson

Project Editors
Mark Janousek
Sally M. Scott

Technical Reviewer
Farhad Dhabhar

Production Coordinator
Todd Halvorsen

Cover Designer
Laura Wellander

The Coriolis Group, LLC • 14455 North Hayden Road, Suite 220 • Scottsdale, Arizona 85260

A Note from Coriolis

Our goal has always been to provide you with the best study tools on the planet to help you achieve your certification in record time. Time is so valuable these days that none of us can afford to waste a second of it, especially when it comes to exam preparation.

Over the past few years, we've created an extensive line of *Exam Cram* and *Exam Prep* study guides, practice exams, and interactive training. To help you study even better, we have now created an e-learning and certification destination called **ExamCram.com**. (You can access the site at **www.examcram.com**.) Now, with every study product you purchase from us, you'll be connected to a large community of people like yourself who are actively studying for their certifications, developing their careers, seeking advice, and sharing their insights and stories.

We believe that the future is all about collaborative learning. Our **ExamCram.com** destination is our approach to creating a highly interactive, easily accessible collaborative environment, where you can take practice exams and discuss your experiences with others, sign up for features like "Questions of the Day," plan your certifications using our interactive planners, create your own personal study pages, and keep up with all of the latest study tips and techniques.

We hope that whatever study products you purchase from us—*Exam Cram* or *Exam Prep* study guides, *Personal Trainers*, *Personal Test Centers*, or one of our interactive Web courses—will make your studying fun and productive. Our commitment is to build the kind of learning tools that will allow you to study the way you want to, whenever you want to.

Visit ExamCram.com now to enhance your study program.

Help us continue to provide the very best certification study materials possible. Write us or email us at **learn@examcram.com** and let us know how our study products have helped you study. Tell us about new features that you'd like us to add. Send us a story about how we've helped you. We're listening!

Good luck with your certification exam and your career. Thank you for allowing us to help you achieve your goals.

ExamCram.com Connects You to the Ultimate Study Center!

Look for these other products from The Coriolis Group:

Mac OS X Version 10.1 Black Book
By Mark R. Bell and Debrah D. Suggs

Mac OS X Version 10.1 Little Black Book
By Gene Steinberg

Mac OS 9.1 Black Book
By Mark R. Bell and Debrah Suggs

Look for these other products from The Coriolis Group:

MCSE Windows XP Professional Exam Prep
By Michael D. Stewart and Neall Alcott

MCSE Windows XP Professional Exam Cram
By Dan Balter and Derek Melber

A+ Practice Tests Exam Cram, Second Edition
By Mike Pastore

CCNA Exam Cram, Third Edition
By Sheldon Barry

To my beautiful wife and daughter, for without you I would be nothing …
—Samuel A. Litt

About the Author

Samuel A. Litt has been employed in the field of personal computing since 1986, working his way up from stock boy at the original Computer Land in Paramus, New Jersey. He has had the good fortune of holding the positions of Creative Technology Manager for MVBMS, as well as IT Director for TBWA/Chiat/Day's New York City office. He is currently employed as the Director of Information Technology for the Blue Rock Editing Company, Manhattan's largest television commercial editorial company. Sam is an Apple-certified technician, an Apple Solution Expert, and a member of the Apple Developer Connection's Select Program.

Acknowledgments

I would like to acknowledge the following people and organizations for their invaluable contributions:

Mr. David J. Rosen Esq.
Sharon Linsenbach
Mark Janousek
Sally M. Scott
Todd Halvorsen
Laura Wellander
Farhad Dhabhar
Emmett Lennon
Jodi M. Litt
Craig Zimmerman
Kevin Boland
Scott Schaefer
Andrew Montgomery
Ted Dunn
The Blue Rock Editing Company
Everyone at The Coriolis Group

Without your kindness and generosity, this project would be naught. Thank you from the bottom of my heart.
—*Samuel A. Litt*

Table of Contents

Introduction

Welcome to *Mac OS X Administration Basics Exam Cram*. This book will help you in preparing to take—and pass—the first of the two-part series of exams for the Apple Certified Technical Coordinator (ACTC) certification. In this introduction, I'll talk about Apple's certification programs and how the *Exam Cram* series can help you prepare for Apple's certification exams.

Exam Cram books help you understand and focus on the subjects and materials you will need in order to pass Apple's certification exams. These books are aimed strictly at test preparation and review and do not teach you everything you need to know about a topic. Instead, they present and dissect the questions and problems you're likely to encounter on a test.

To completely prepare yourself for the Mac OS X Administration Basics Exam, I recommend that you begin by taking Apple's Mac OS X skills assessment at the following URL:

http://a1568.g.akamai.net/7/1568/51/4bbcefeb563955/www.apple.com/iservices/certification/pdf/AdminBasics_SAG_060101c.pdf

In order to view this document, you will need Adobe Acrobat Reader. This guide will help you evaluate your knowledge base against Apple's own requirements for the test.

Based on what you learn from that exercise, you might decide to begin your studies with some classroom training or by reading one of the several OS X how-to books available from The Coriolis Group or other third-party vendors. I also strongly recommend that you install, configure, and work with the software you'll be tested on, because nothing beats hands-on experience and familiarity when it comes to understanding the questions you're likely to encounter on a certification test. Book learning is essential, but hands-on experience is the best teacher of all.

The Apple Certified Technical Coordinator (ACTC) Certification

Apple states that "Apple Certified Technical Coordinator (ACTC) certification is ideal for a traditional Mac and AppleShare IP user who may not be a full-time professional system administrator but who is tasked with maintaining a modest network of machines. Typical technical coordinators are teachers and school technology specialists, designated power users within larger organizations, or helpdesk personnel."

Apple intends to have a second certification, the Apple Certified System Administrator (ACSA) that is "designed for full-time professional system administrators managing medium-to-large networks of Mac systems in demanding and relatively complex multiplatform deployments." This certification is composed of five exams, with an emphasis on Apple's server and networking technologies. At the time of this book's publication, the Apple Certified System Administrator (ACSA) certification was not to be available until the spring of 2000.

The ACTC certification is composed of two separate tests:

➤ *Mac OS X Administration Basics (Exam 9L0-500)*—This is the base test for both the ACTC and the ACSA certifications. The knowledge that is tested in this exam will serve as the foundation for all OS X certification tests. This test focuses on the fundamentals of OS X design and operation and tests the core knowledge necessary for maintaining an OS X system.

➤ *Mac OS X Server Essentials (Exam 9l0-501)*—This test focuses on the essentials for managing Mac OS X Server and integrating it into the network of Mac OS systems.

To obtain ACTC certification, you must pass both exams. You do not have to take the tests in any particular order, although I would recommend taking the Mac OS X Administration Basics exam first.

It's not uncommon for the entire process to take a couple of months. Do not get deterred if you must take a test more than once to pass. The primary goal of the *Exam Cram* series is to make it possible, given proper study and preparation, to pass both of the required ACTC tests on the first try.

Finally, certification is an ongoing activity. Once an OS X version becomes obsolete, you will need to get recertified on the current product version. Because technology keeps changing and new products continually supplant old ones, this should come as no surprise.

The best place to keep tabs on the ACTC program and its certification exams is on the Apple Web site. The current root URL for the ACTC program is **www.apple.com/iservices/technicaltraining/**. This will help you find the latest and most accurate information about Apple's certification programs.

Taking a Certification Exam

Alas, testing is not free. You'll be charged $150 for each test you take, whether you pass or fail. In the United States and Canada, Prometric administers the tests. Prometric can be reached at 1-888-APL-EXAM (1-888-275-3926), any time from 7:00 A.M. to 6:00 P.M., Central Time, Monday through Friday. You can also visit their Web site at **www.prometric.com** for testing center location and registration information.

To schedule an exam, call at least one day in advance. To cancel or reschedule an exam, you must call at least one day before the scheduled test time (otherwise, you might be charged the $150 fee). When calling Prometric, be sure to have the following information ready:

➤ Your name, organization, and mailing address.

➤ The name of the exam you want to take.

➤ A method of payment. (The most convenient approach is to supply a valid credit card number with sufficient available credit. Otherwise, payments by check, money order, or purchase order must be received before a test can be scheduled. If one of the latter methods is required, ask the representative for more details.)

An appointment confirmation will be sent to you by mail (if you register more than five days before an exam) or by fax (if fewer than five days). A Candidate Agreement letter, which you must sign to take the examination, will also be provided.

On the day of the test, try to arrive at least 15 minutes before the scheduled time. You must supply two forms of identification, one of which must be a photo ID.

All exams are completely closed book. In fact, you will not be permitted to take anything with you into the testing area. I suggest that you review the most critical information about your test immediately prior to entering the room. (*Exam Cram* books provide a brief reference—the Cram Sheet, located inside the front of this book—that lists in distilled form the essential information from the book.) You will have some time to compose yourself, to mentally review this critical information, and even to take a sample orientation exam before you begin the real thing. I suggest you take the orientation test before your first exam. Both exams are more or less identical in layout, behavior, and controls, so you probably won't need to do this after the first test.

When you complete an ACTC certification exam, the testing software will tell you whether you've passed or failed. Results are broken into several topic areas. Whether you pass or fail, you should receive—and keep—a detailed report that the test administrator prints for you. You can use the report to help you prepare for another go-round, if necessary. If you pass, you can use the report to see the areas you should review to keep your edge. If you need to retake an exam, you'll have to call Prometric, schedule a new test date, and pay another $150.

Tracking ACTC Status

After you pass both exams, you'll be certified as an Apple Certified Technical Coordinator. Once certified, you will receive an ACTC certificate suitable for framing. Official certification might take anywhere from four to six weeks (although generally four weeks), so don't expect to get your credentials overnight.

Apple lists the following as the benefits of ACTC certification:

➤ Technical credibility

➤ Better problem-solving skills

➤ Greater job satisfaction through increased technical competency

➤ Recognition by peers within the industry

How to Prepare for an Exam

At a minimum, preparing for the Mac OS X Administration Basics exam requires that you obtain and study the following materials:

➤ An OS X–compatible Macintosh computer.

➤ The latest version of OS X.

➤ This *Exam Cram* book. (It's the first and last thing you should read before taking the exam.)

In addition, you'll probably find the following useful in your quest for Mac OS X Administration expertise:

➤ *Classroom training*—Apple, as well as several other companies, offers classroom training that you might find helpful in preparing for the exam. But a word of warning: These classes are fairly expensive (in the range of $2000 per class). The exams are closely tied to the classroom training provided by Apple, so taking these classes to achieve the ACTC certification is almost a sure thing.

➤ *Other publications*—You will find direct references to other publications and resources in this book, and there's no shortage of materials available about OS X Administration Basics topics. To help you sift through some of the publications out there, each chapter ends with a "Need to Know More?" section that provides pointers to additional resources covering that chapter's subject matter.

About This Book

Each *Exam Cram* chapter follows a regular structure, along with graphical cues about especially important or useful material. Here's the structure of a typical chapter:

➤ *Introduction*—Each chapter begins with an outline of concepts and associated terminology that you must learn and understand before you can be fully conversant with the chapter's subject matter. I conclude this section with one or two introductory paragraphs to set the stage for the rest of the chapter.

➤ *Topical coverage*—After the opening lists, each chapter covers a series of topics related to its subject matter.

All the contents of this book are associated, at least tangentially, to something test related. This book is tightly focused for quick test preparation, so you'll find that what appears in the meat of each chapter is critical knowledge.

➤ *Practice questions*—This section presents a series of mock test questions and explanations of both correct and incorrect answers.

➤ *Review and additional resources*—This section at the end of each chapter provides direct pointers to Apple and third-party resources that offer further details on the chapter's subject matter.

The bulk of the book slavishly follows this chapter structure, but I would like to point out a few other elements. Chapter 10 includes a sample test that provides a good review of the material presented throughout the book to ensure you're ready for the exam. Chapter 11 provides an answer key to the sample test. Additionally, you'll find a glossary and an index that you can use to define and track down terms as they appear in the text.

Finally, look for the Cram Sheet, which appears inside the front of this *Exam Cram* book, because it is a valuable tool that represents a condensed and compiled collection of facts, figures, and tips that I think you should memorize before taking the test. Because you can dump this information out of your head onto a piece of paper before answering any exam questions, you can master this information by brute force, remembering it only long enough to write it down after you walk into the test room. You might even want to look at it in the car or in the lobby of the testing center just before you walk in to take the test.

How to Use This Book

If you're prepping for a first-time test, I've structured the topics in this book to build upon each other. Therefore, some topics in later chapters make more sense if you've read earlier chapters. That's why I suggest you read this book from front to back for your initial test preparation.

If you need to brush up on a topic or have to prepare for a second try, use the index or table of contents to find the topics and questions you need to study. Beyond the tests, I think you'll find this book useful as a tightly focused reference to some of the most important concepts associated with the Mac OS X Administration Basics exam.

Given the entire book's elements and its specialized focus, I've tried to create a tool that you can use to prepare for—and especially to pass—the Mac OS X Administration Basics exam. Please share your feedback on the book with me, especially if you have ideas about how I can improve it for future test-takers. I'll consider everything you say carefully, and I'll try to respond to all suggestions and questions. You can reach me via email at **salitt@mac.com**, or you can send your questions or comments to **learn@examcram.com**. Please remember to use the title of the book in your message; otherwise, we'll be forced to guess which book you're writing about. And we don't like to guess—we want to *know*! Also, be sure to check out the Web pages at **www.examcram.com** where you'll find information, updates, commentary, and certification information.

Thanks, and enjoy the book!

Mac OS X Administration Basics Certification Exam

Terms you'll need to understand:

- ✓ Radio button
- ✓ Checkbox
- ✓ Exhibit
- ✓ Multiple-choice question formats
- ✓ Process of elimination

Techniques you'll need to master:

- ✓ Assessing your exam-readiness
- ✓ Preparing to take a certification exam
- ✓ Practicing (to make perfect)
- ✓ Mastering the art of careful reading
- ✓ Making the best use of the testing software
- ✓ Budgeting your time
- ✓ Saving the hardest questions until last
- ✓ Guessing (as a last resort)

As experiences go, taking tests is not something that most people eagerly look forward to, no matter how well prepared they are. In most cases, however, familiarity helps ameliorate test anxiety. In plain English, this means you probably won't be as nervous when you take your fourth or fifth Apple certification exam as you will be when you take your first.

Whether it's your first test or your tenth, understanding the exam-taking particulars (how much time to spend on questions, the setting you'll be in, and so on) and the testing software will help you concentrate on the material rather than on the environment. Likewise, mastering a few basic test-taking skills should help you recognize—and perhaps even outfox—some of the tricks you're bound to find on the Mac OS X Administration Basics exam.

This chapter is going to cover the testing environment and software, as well as some proven test-taking strategies you should be able to use to your advantage.

Assessing Exam-Readiness

Before you take the Mac OS X Administration Basics exam, I strongly recommend that you read through and take the self-assessment material Apple provides, which can be found at the following URL:

http://a1568.g.akamai.net/7/1568/51/4bbcefeb563955/www.apple.com/ iservices/certification/pdf/AdminBasics_SAG_060101c.pdf

In order to view this document, you will need Adobe Acrobat Reader. This guide will help you evaluate your knowledge base against Apple's own requirements for the test. It will help you compare your existing knowledge base to the requirements for passing the exam.

Once you've gone through the self-assessment, you can address those areas where your background or experience might not measure up to that of an ideal certification candidate. However, you can also tackle subject matter for individual tests at the same time, so you can continue making progress while you're catching up in some areas.

Once you've worked through this *Exam Cram*, read the supplementary materials, and taken the practice test at the end of the book, you'll have a pretty clear idea of when you should be ready to take the real exam. Although you will only need to keep practicing until your score tops the 75 percent mark, 85 percent would be a good goal to give yourself some margin for error in a real exam situation (where stress will play more of a role than when you practice). Once you hit that point, you should be ready to go. However, if you get through the practice exam in this book without attaining that score, you should work with the questions, keep taking practice tests, and study the materials until you get there.

The Testing Situation

When you arrive at the Prometric testing center where you've scheduled your test, you'll need to sign in with a test coordinator. You'll be asked to produce two forms of identification, one of which must be a photo ID. Once you've signed in and your time slot arrives, you'll be asked to leave any books, bags, or other items you brought with you, and you'll be escorted into a closed room. Typically, the room will be furnished with one to six computers, and each workstation will be separated from the others by dividers designed to keep you from seeing what's happening on someone else's computer.

You'll be furnished with a pen or pencil and a blank sheet of paper or, in some cases, an erasable plastic sheet with an erasable felt-tip pen. You're allowed to write down any information you want on this sheet. I suggest that you memorize as much as possible of the material that appears on the Cram Sheet (inside the front cover of this book) and then write down that information on the blank sheet as soon as you sit in front of the test machine. You can refer to the sheet any time you like during the test, but you'll have to surrender it when you leave the room.

Most test rooms feature a wall with a large window from which the test coordinator will monitor the room. The test coordinator will have loaded the test you've signed up for—Mac OS X Administration Basics (Exam 9L0-500)—and you'll be permitted to start as soon as you're seated in front of the machine.

The exam has an allotted time limit of 90 minutes. The computer maintains an onscreen counter/clock so that you can check the time remaining any time you like. The exam essentially consists of 80 questions. There are approximately five statistical/demographic questions at the beginning of the exam. An example of such a question is "How did you study for this exam?"

Note: The passing score for the Mac OS X Administration Basics exam is 75 percent. You must get 60 questions correct out of 80 total questions.

The Mac OS X Administration Basics exam is computer administered (on a PC—the irony) and uses a multiple-choice/fill-in-the-blank format. Although this might sound easy, the questions are constructed not just to check your mastery of basic facts but also to evaluate your operational knowledge of the OS. More complex questions might include so-called *exhibits*, which may come in the form of a table or a chart of some sort. Paying careful attention to such exhibits is the key to success. Use your sheet of paper to write down notes on the questions that you find complicated—such notes might help in the process of eliminating incorrect answers. In order to answer the questions, you will be required to position your mouse over the radio button next to the appropriate answer and click the mouse to select that choice.

The Anatomy of the Test

The test is broken down into the following sections:

➤ Installation and Interface (4 items)

➤ User Accounts (10 items)

➤ File System (9 items)

➤ Application Support (10 items)

➤ Classic Support (8 items)

➤ Networking (11 items)

➤ File Sharing (6 items)

➤ Device Support (1 item)

➤ Administrative Functions (8 items)

➤ Command Line (4 items)

➤ Problem Solving (9 items)

As you can see, some sections are emphasized more than others. In the next eight chapters, I will share with you my personal insights and knowledge I have gained from my Mac OS X Administration Basics exam preparation experience.

Using Prometric's Test Software Effectively

A well-known test-taking strategy is first to read over the entire test from start to finish, but to answer only those questions you feel absolutely sure of on this pass. On subsequent passes, you can dive into more complex questions, knowing how many such questions you have remaining and the time you have to spend on those questions.

Fortunately, the Prometric test software makes this approach easy to implement. At the top of each screen, you'll find a checkbox that permits you to mark that question for a later visit. (Note that marking questions makes review easier, but you can return to any question by clicking the Forward or Back button repeatedly until you get to the question.) As you read each question, if you answer only those you're sure of and mark for review those you're not sure of, you can keep going through a decreasing list of open questions as you knock off the trickier ones in order.

There's at least one potential benefit to reading through the test before answering the trickier questions. Sometimes you find information in later questions that sheds light on earlier ones. Other times, information you read in later questions might jog your memory about OS X's facts, figures, or behaviors that also will help with earlier questions. Either way, you'll come out ahead if you defer those questions about which you're not absolutely sure.

Keep working on the questions until you are absolutely sure of all your answers or until you know you'll run out of time. If you still have unanswered questions and time is running out, you'll want to zip through them and guess. Not answering a question at all guarantees only that you'll get no credit for it, and a guess has at least a chance of being correct (*Prometric scores blank answers and incorrect answers as equally wrong*).

Taking Testing Seriously

The most important advice I can give you about taking any test is this: Read each question carefully. Some questions are deliberately ambiguous; some use double negatives; others use terminology in incredibly precise ways. I've taken numerous practice tests and real tests, and I've found that it is very easy to misread a question or to read something into a question that is beyond what is being asked.

Here are some suggestions on how to deal with the tendency to jump to an answer too quickly:

➤ Make sure you read every word in the question. If you find yourself jumping ahead impatiently, return to the beginning of the question and start over.

➤ As you read, try to restate the question in your own terms. If you can do this, you should be able to pick the correct answer(s) much more easily.

➤ When returning to a question after your initial read-through, reread every word again. Otherwise, your mind might fall quickly into a rut. Sometimes seeing a question afresh after turning your attention elsewhere lets you see something you missed before, but the strong tendency is to see only what you've seen before. Try to avoid this natural tendency at all times.

➤ If you return to a question more than twice, try to articulate to yourself what you don't understand about the question, why the answers don't appear to make sense, or what appears to be missing. If you chew on the subject for a while, your subconscious might provide the details that are lacking, or you might notice a "trick" that will point to the right answer.

Question-Handling Strategies

Based on the tests I've taken, a couple of interesting trends in the answers have become apparent. For those questions that take only a single answer, usually two or three of the answers will be obviously incorrect, and two of the answers will be plausible. But, of course, only one can be correct. Unless the answer leaps out at you (and if it does, reread the question to look for a trick, because sometimes those are the ones you're most likely to get wrong), begin the answering process by eliminating those that are obviously wrong.

Things to look for in the "obviously wrong" category include spurious command choices or table or view names, nonexistent software or command options, and terminology you've never seen before. If you've done your homework for a test, no valid information should be completely new to you. In that case, unfamiliar or bizarre terminology probably indicates a totally bogus answer.

When dealing with questions that require multiple answers, you must know and select all of the correct options to get credit. This, too, qualifies as an example of why careful reading is so important.

As you work your way through the test, another counter that Prometric provides will come in handy: a tally of questions completed and questions outstanding. Budget your time by making sure you've completed one-fourth of the questions one-quarter of the way through the test period (between 14 and 15 questions in the first 22 or 23 minutes). Check again three-quarters of the way through (between 44 and 45 questions in the first 66 to 69 minutes).

If you're not through after 85 minutes, use the last 5 minutes to guess your way through the remaining questions. Remember that guesses are potentially more valuable than blank answers, because blanks are always wrong, and a guess might turn out to be right. If you haven't a clue about any of the remaining questions, pick answers at random. The important thing is to submit a test for scoring that has an answer for every question.

 At the very end of your test period, you're better off guessing than leaving questions blank or unanswered. If you have to guess, go with your first impression because that is often the correct answer.

Mastering the Inner Game

In the final analysis, knowledge breeds confidence, and confidence breeds success. If you study the materials in this book carefully and review all the questions at the end of each chapter, you should be aware of those areas for which additional studying is required.

Next, follow up by reading some or all of the materials recommended in the "Need to Know More?" section at the end of each chapter. The idea is to become familiar enough with the concepts and situations you find in the sample questions to be able to reason your way through similar situations on a real test. If you know the material, you have every right to be confident that you can pass the test.

Once you've worked your way through the book, take the practice test in Chapter 10. The test will provide a reality check and will help you identify areas that you need to study further. Make sure you follow up and review materials related to the questions you miss before scheduling a real test. Only when you've covered all the ground and feel comfortable with the whole scope of the practice test should you take a real test.

 If you take the sample test (Chapter 10) and you don't score at least 80 percent correct, you'll want to practice further. As with any sample test, you need to beware of becoming so familiar with the test itself that you are answering the questions by rote. If you find yourself answering the questions before you finish reading them, you have become too familiar with the test, and the format is no longer helpful.

Armed with the information in this book and with the determination to increase your knowledge, you should be able to pass the certification exam. But, if you don't work at it, you'll spend the test fee more than once before you finally do pass. If you prepare seriously, the exam should go flawlessly. Good luck!

Coping with Change on the Web

Sooner or later, all the specifics I've shared with you about the Web-based resources I mention throughout this book will go stale or will be replaced by newer information. In some cases, the URLs you find here might lead you to their replacements; in other cases, URLs will go nowhere, leaving you with the dreaded "404 File not found" error message.

When that happens, please don't give up. There's always a way to find what you want on the Web, if you're willing to invest some time and energy. To begin with, most large or complex Web sites—and Apple's qualifies on both counts—offer search engines. As long as you can get to Apple's home page (and I'm sure that it will stay at **www.apple.com** for a long while yet), you can use this tool to help you find what you need.

Finally, don't be afraid to use general search engine tools such as **www.google.com** to search for related information. So, if you can't find something where this book says it lives, start looking around. If worse comes to worst, you can always email me! My email address is **salitt@mac.com**.

 Do not get too wrapped up in the technical issues of Mac OS X because the exam is more about being an OS X expert user than being a troubleshooter. In your efforts to achieve exam success, make sure to take a balanced approach between conceptual knowledge and practical know-how.

Introduction to OS X

Terms you'll need to understand:
- ✓ Darwin
- ✓ Quartz
- ✓ OpenGL
- ✓ QuickTime
- ✓ Aqua
- ✓ Classic
- ✓ Mach 3.0 microkernel

Techniques you'll need to master:
- ✓ Knowing the history of OS X
- ✓ Mastering the buzz-word-enabled core technologies of OS X

Mac OS X is Apple's answer to the quest for a modern operating system (OS). It combines the power and stability of UNIX with the simplicity of the Macintosh. In 1996, as a result of many internal failed attempts to develop a next-generation operating system, Apple management looked outside the company and acquired NeXT Software Inc. NeXT's OS at the time was called OpenStep. It had all the features that Apple desired in a modern OS: protected memory, preemptive multitasking, multithreading, and symmetric multiprocessing. With OpenStep as the foundation, Apple initially designated the code name Rhapsody for its new OS; as the project moved forward and matured, however, it was later renamed OS X, keeping in line with the progression of Apple's existing system software monikers.

Before we delve into this chapter's material, you should already be somewhat familiar with the technologies that underlie OS 9, although it is not essential to have an in-depth knowledge to pass the exam. As for knowing the complexities of Unix, there is very little you will need to master in order to pass the Mac OS X Administration Basics exam. If you are worried about recanting complex Unix commands, fear not—there are only a couple of command-line questions on the exam.

This chapter will go over the core technologies that make up OS X. It is important to have an understanding of these core technologies. Having a familiarity with the core system technologies will provide an excellent foundation for the comprehension of all exam material. Remember, this book is a study guide for passing the Mac OS X Administration Basics exam (Exam 9L0-500), not a how-to guide for the operation of OS X. This book does assume that you already own a copy of OS X and a compatible Macintosh computer and that you already have some exposure to the OS X operating system.

Under the Hood of OS X

If OS X were to be compared to a car engine, we would see a similarity in that both are composed of many parts. All these parts have very distinct functions, and they all make up a greater whole. The intention of Apple was to build an engine akin to a Formula 1 racecar engine. When the engineers at Apple set out to build OS X, they pulled together world-class technologies in an effort to build the most advanced consumer operating system the world had ever seen.

Note: The one thing that Apple wants the world to know about Mac OS X is that it is based on open standards. This is because at the heart of OS X is Unix, which has played a major role in the development of the Internet. Because Unix is so "Internet centric," this allows OS X to be integrated in virtually any computing environment.

Darwin

The foundation of OS X is Darwin, which is an Open Source community/Apple joint effort. The primary objective of the Darwin project is to build an industrial-strength Unix-based operating system core that will provide greater stability and performance compared to the existing iterations of the Mac OS to date. To review Darwin in detail is beyond the scope of this book. Instead, we shall review some of Darwin's more marketed features.

Mach 3.0 Microkernel

At the center of Darwin is the Mach 3.0 microkernel, which provides the basic services for all other parts of the operating system. Mach was developed at Carnegie-Mellon University, and it has a closely tied history with BSD Unix (Berkeley Software Distribution). It is Mach that gives OS X the features of protected memory architecture, preemptive multitasking, and symmetric multiprocessing.

Protected Memory

Protected memory isolates applications in their own individual memory workspaces. In the event of an application crash, the program can be terminated without having a negative effect on other running applications or requiring a restart of the computer.

Advance Memory Management

Advance Memory Management automatically manages physical RAM and virtual memory dynamically as needed. Virtual memory utilizes hard disk space in lieu of physical RAM. Information that would normally sit in RAM, but is not currently needed, is transferred to the hard disk in order to free up physical RAM for the demands of data/applications that do need it. This eliminates the need for users of previous Macintosh desktop operating systems from having to manually adjust memory allocations; it also alleviates out-of-memory conditions.

Preemptive Multitasking

Preemptive multitasking prioritizes processor tasks by order of importance. It allows the computer to handle multiple tasks simultaneously. This method of managing processor tasks more efficiently allows the computer to remain responsive, even during the most processor-intensive tasks.

Symmetric Multiprocessing

Symmetric multiprocessing provides support for multiprocessor Macintosh computer systems. This will allow developers to build applications that take advantage of two or more processors by assigning applications to a specific processor or by splitting an application's tasks between multiple processors simultaneously.

It is the Darwin foundation that provides greater stability and the performance necessary for OS X to be considered an industrial-strength modern operating system.

Quartz

Quartz is a powerful two-dimensional (2D) graphics-rendering system. It has built-in support for the Portable Document Format (PDF), on-the-fly rendering, compositing, and antialiasing. It supports multiple font formats, including TrueType, Postscript Type 1, and OpenType. Quartz supports Apple's ColorSync color-management technology, allowing for consistent and accurate color in the print/graphics environment.

OpenGL

Open Graphics Library (OpenGL) started out as a technology initiative by Silicon Graphics Inc., a manufacturer of high-end graphics workstations. It has since become an industry standard for three-dimensional (3D) graphics rendering. It provides a standard graphics Application Programming Interface (API) by which software and hardware manufacturers can build 3D applications and hardware across multiple platforms on a common standard. OpenGL is prevalent in gaming, computer-aided design (CAD), professional 3D animation/modeling, and graphic design.

QuickTime

QuickTime is Apple's cross-platform multimedia authoring and distribution engine. It is both a file format and a suite of applications. QuickTime has been around since 1991 and has matured into a very powerful technology. QuickTime supports more than 50 media file formats encompassing audio, video and still images. Some examples of these formats include AIFF, AVI, JPEG, MIDI, MP3, MPEG-1, PICT, and TIFF, to name a few. QuickTime has support for real-time video streaming, allowing viewers to tune in to live or prerecorded content on demand.

Aqua

Aqua is Mac OS X's new graphical user interface (GUI). It is a dramatic departure from OS 9's Platinum interface, although it retains certain common elements. This allows for greater interface familiarity for legacy Macintosh operators, making the transition to OS X a more intuitive experience. The Aqua interface consists of many new graphical elements. Although this book does not have a chapter dedicated solely to the Aqua GUI, it will be touched on throughout the book.

Classic

In the world of OS X, Classic is what is referred to as a *compatibility environment*. Classic provides OS X with the ability to run a full version of Mac OS 9 in a protected memory space. This compatibility environment allows the user to run most Macintosh legacy software that has not been updated to run natively in OS X. As a result of the power of Darwin, in the event that an offending program within Classic causes the Application Environment to crash, the system software safely terminates the process without negative consequences for other running OS X applications.

Note: The preceding was a brief review of some of the more heavily marketed buzz-word-enabled technologies that make up OS X. If you are interested in obtaining further information, consult the "Need to Know More?" section at the end of this chapter for additional resources.

Practice Questions

Question 1

> Which technology is the foundation of OS X?
>
> ○ a. Cocoa
>
> ○ b. Quartz
>
> ○ c. Mach
>
> ○ d. OpenGL

Answer c is correct. Mach is the core technology that provides basic services for all parts of the operating system. Answer a is incorrect because Cocoa is an OS X application environment; it will be reviewed in Chapter 4. Answer b is incorrect because Quartz is OS X's 2D graphics engine. Answer d is incorrect because OpenGL is OS X's 3D graphics engine.

Question 2

> Which of the following technologies are components of Quartz? [Check all correct answers]
>
> ❏ a. QuickTime
>
> ❏ b. Carbon
>
> ❏ c. Portable Document Format
>
> ❏ d. ColorSync

Answers c and d are correct. Portable Document Format (PDF) is the rendering engine of OS X. It enables OS X–native applications to embed, manipulate, and even save data as PDF documents. ColorSync is Apple's color-management technology, which allows for consistent and accurate color in the print/graphics environment. Answer a is incorrect because QuickTime is Apple's cross-platform multimedia authoring and distribution engine. Answer b is incorrect because Carbon is an OS X application environment; it will be reviewed in Chapter 4.

Question 3

> OpenGL is an industry standard for which applications? [Check all correct answers]
>
> ❑ a. Desktop video
>
> ❑ b. Gaming
>
> ❑ c. Modeling and animation
>
> ❑ d. Desktop publishing

Answers b and c are correct. OpenGL is an industry standard for three-dimensional (3D) graphics rendering. OpenGL technology is heavily utilized within the industries of professional graphics/animation and 3D gaming. Answers a and d are incorrect because OpenGL does not play a significant role in desktop video or desktop publishing applications.

Question 4

> Which item listed below is the technology responsible for multimedia authoring?
>
> ○ a. QuickTime
>
> ○ b. Symmetric Multiprocessing
>
> ○ c. Protected Memory
>
> ○ d. Aqua

Answer a is correct. For the past 10 years, Apple has relied on QuickTime as its cross-platform multimedia authoring and distribution engine. Answer b is incorrect because symmetric multiprocessing allows software to take advantage of multiprocessor hardware designs. Answer c is incorrect because protected memory isolates applications into their own individual workspaces. Answer d is incorrect because Aqua is the designation for OS X's new GUI.

Question 5

Aqua is the name that Apple uses to refer to which technology?

○ a. 2D onscreen rasterizing

○ b. Symmetric multiprocessing

○ c. Protected memory

○ d. GUI

○ e. Mach 3.0 microkernel

Answer d is correct. Aqua is the designation that Apple has assigned for OS X's GUI. Aqua is a bold step forward in interface design, although it still feels intuitive to the Mac user as a result of retaining familiar graphical elements from OS 9's Platinum interface. Answer a is incorrect because 2D onscreen rasterizing is handled by Quartz. Answer b is incorrect because symmetric multiprocessing allows software to take advantage of multiprocessor hardware designs. Answer c is incorrect because protected memory isolates applications into their own individual workspaces. Answer e is incorrect because the Mach 3.0 microkernel is the foundation of Mac OS X and provides basic services for all other parts of the operating system.

Question 6

True or false: In the event that Classic crashes, OS X will require a restart.

○ a. True

○ b. False

Answer b is correct. Classic takes advantage of the Mach microkernel's protected memory spaces feature. As a result, when the Classic environment crashes, other running applications are unaffected; this alleviates the necessity of a system restart.

Need to Know More?

 The Apple Developer Web site is a great source of Mac OS X theoretical knowledge. It can be found at **http://developer.apple.com/macosx**.

 For more information in regard to Apple's Open Source initiatives check out **www.opensource.apple.com**.

 Visit the Mach Project home page, a one-stop shop for everything Mach. It can be found at **www.cs.cmu.edu/afs/cs.cmu.edu/project/ mach/public/www/mach.html**.

Installation of Mac OS X

Terms you'll need to understand:

✓ Firmware

✓ Partition

✓ Base system software

✓ Essential system software

✓ BSD subsystem

✓ iTools

✓ Software update

Techniques you'll need to master:

✓ Understanding the hardware requirements

✓ Knowing the installation options

✓ Configuring the Setup Assistant

✓ Comprehending advantages and limitations of Mac OS X's disk format options

Now that we have reviewed the core technologies of Mac OS X, let's focus on its installation process. This chapter will cover the installation requirements and the available installation options.

Although Mac OS X has a very structured install process, several variations of installation are available. The user's needs will dictate the appropriate installation strategy. However, before any Mac OS X implementation can take place, it is necessary to evaluate the target computer to see whether it meets Apple's official hardware requirements.

Hardware Requirements of OS X

Apple's minimum hardware requirements for Mac OS X includes a factory-shipped G3 Macintosh CPU with 128MB of RAM, an Apple-supplied video card, and 1.5GB of available hard disk space. This roughly translates to all Beige G3 hardware and up, as well as video display cards/options that were shipped from Apple's factory. The Apple factory-shipped video display cards/options are ixMicro, ATI, and NVIDIA. As for third-party hardware, Apple states that OS X includes support for many third-party hardware devices, although some devices may need additional driver support/updates from their respective manufacturers. The only exception to the minimum requirement of a factory-shipped Macintosh G3 is the original PowerBook G3. This machine is unsupported and can be distinguished from other PowerBook G3 machines by its resemblance to the PowerBook 3400. It has a six-color Apple logo on the top cover of the display, and the identification sticker on the bottom of the computer states that its family number is (M3553).

Preparing for the Installation of OS X

Once you have decided that the target hardware meets OS X's minimum hardware requirements, you will need to verify that the target computer's firmware is up to date. Simply stated, firmware is programming that tells a computer's hardware how to behave. Starting with the iMac, Macintosh computers have utilized a firmware-upgradeable hardware design. This design element is a component of what is referred to as *NewWorld Architecture*. The Power Mac's firmware is inserted into a programmable (flashable) read-only memory (PROM). This programmable firmware approach enables Apple to fix technical issues via updates like any other software. As a result, this innovation allows Apple to achieve greater hardware stability and overall improved system performance. Using a utility referred to as a Flash-ROM updater, firmware can be upgraded (sometimes referred to as *revved*). Apple's latest firmware can be obtained through either the Software Update Control Panel of Mac OS 9 or the following Web address, **www.info.apple.com/support/downloads.html**.

The only Apple-supported OS X Macintosh computers that do not contain NewWorld Architecture are Beige G3 Power Macs and G3 Series Wall Street PowerBooks. The WallStreet PowerBook can be distinguished from other G3 Series PowerBooks by the lack of a bronze/semitranslucent keyboard.

Installation Strategies for OS X

OS X has three installation strategies, each with its own advantages and disadvantages. Common to all three installation strategies is the requirement that the install partition needs to be formatted as an Extended (HFS+) volume. An HFS+ formatted volume's single biggest advantage is that it is "case preserving." All Macintosh desktop OSs to date have utilized file systems that have been dependent on case-preserving formatted volumes (this includes the old HFS format as well).

The opposite of the case-preserving format is the case-sensitive format. With the case-sensitive format, it is possible to have multiple files named identically in the same location/folder/directory. The only thing that would differentiate the files to the naked eye is the varied use of uppercase characters. For example, it is possible to have individual files named DOG, DoG, Dog, dOg, doG, dOG, and dog located in the same folder. Because Apple ships all OS 9 computers as HFS+, this will provide the most transparent path for file migration to OS X.

OS X also supports another format referred to as the Unix File System (UFS), although it isn't the preferred format because it does not support AirPort networking and is case sensitive. In addition, UFS volumes do not show up when booted from Mac OS 9, their volume names cannot be customized, and special attention (extra effort) is needed in order to run Classic from a UFS volume. One more important limitation to know about the UFS format is that Mac OS 9 files may not read correctly when OS X's command line is read. In Chapter 4, we will review Mac OS X's file system in greater detail. Apple states that "a UFS format may be desired for developing Unix-based applications *within* OS X," and you should not choose this format unless you specifically need it. Apple also states that the UFS format should not be used if your Mac OS X installation destination is a *G3 Blue & White*.

It is always a good idea to make a backup of your hard drive before you upgrade system software. This can be accomplished many different ways, but I prefer Dantz's Retrospect Express backup utility. It is also a good idea to verify and repair, if necessary, the integrity of your hard disk's data structure with an industrial-strength repair utility prior to OS X's installation. In this instance, I recommend Alsoft's DiskWarrior or

Symantec's Norton SystemWorks. I personally use a combination of both. If by some chance you don't use one of these hard disk utilities, Mac OS X's installer runs its own check and repairs the integrity of your hard drive as well. However, there may be some instances in which it will be incapable of doing so.

Single Partition

A single-partition installation combines OS X and OS 9 on the same partition/logical volume. Its primary advantage is that it is the quickest and easiest of the Mac OS X installation strategies. An advantage of the single-partition installation is that Mac OS X can be installed on top of an existing Mac OS 9–prepared hard drive. In fact, Apple ships preinstalled OS X Macs as single-partition installation. Another way of building a single-partition installation is by utilizing the Software Restore CDs that come with OS X–preinstalled Macs. These CDs will restore your machine back to the original way it shipped from Apple's factory.

Note: One of the biggest disadvantages of utilizing the Software Restore CDs is that Apple does not take into account software installations and modifications that have occurred since the initial factory preparation. These software installations and modifications can include user preferences and documents as well as third-party applications and system software updates. All this can be accommodated if a backup of the target Mac is made prior to the utilization of the Software Restore CDs and the Mac administrator has the skill and the time to restore the end-user's software modifications.

Separate Partitions

A separate-partitions installation is where OS X and OS 9 are installed on two separate partitions on the same hard drive or on two entirely separate hard disks. The main advantage of the separate partition strategy is that it provides a safety net in the event that the OS X portion becomes damaged. By separating OS 9 and OS X, you can easily erase and reinstall the OS X portion while preserving the OS 9 portion. This modular approach was initially Apple's recommended strategy for OS X installation prior to shipping OS X–preinstalled Macs.

The separate-partitions strategy is probably the safest way to migrate to OS X, although it does require the greatest effort. In order to set up a separate-partitions system, you will need to back up all data on your existing hard disk and reformat it with the most current version of Drive Setup into two partitions.

An alternate way to build a separate-partitions system is to install a second hard drive, if your Mac has built-in support for it. If your Mac does not have built-in support for this, it may be possible to install a second hard drive by means of a third-party OS X–compatible SCSI or IDE PCI host adapter card. Never take for granted that you have the latest firmware for your third-party or Apple-supplied SCSI or IDE PCI host adapter card. You should always check with the manufacturer's Web sites. Finally, installation of OS X on a Universal Serial Bus (USB) or FireWire hard drive is unsupported.

A SCSI chain that works with Mac OS 9 may not work with Mac OS X. AppleCare Knowledge Base article 106147 states that OSX is less tolerant to improper SCSI termination than OS 9.

If a hard disk of greater capacity than 8GB is installed in a Beige PowerMac G3, WallStreet PowerBook, or a Revision A, B, C, D iMac, Mac OS X must be installed within the first 8GB of the primary hard disk.

At this point you will either restore your Mac OS 9 backup or reinstall OS 9 from scratch.

Once the OS 9 portion has been completed, you may proceed to install OS X on the other partition/hard disk.

Note: Apple states in its "Before You Install" document, which can be found on the OS X support site at www.info.apple.com/usen/macosx/, that it is possible to have multiple installations of Mac OS X on the same machine on separate partitions. Further, it was recommended that the newer version of OS X reside on the lower partition. Contradictory to that information is Article 106220 in the AppleCare Knowledge Base. It states that if multiple versions of OS X are installed on the same Mac, the computer may be unable to select a desired startup system folder. Therefore, you should not install multiple instances of Mac OS X on different partitions on the same computer.

Mac OS X Only

A "Mac OS X only" installation is identical to a single-partition installation, with the exception that this install strategy does not include a Mac OS 9 installation. Although this strategy affords the simplicity of supporting one operating system (Mac OS X), be aware that you will be eliminating the option of running the Classic Application Environment.

It is possible to install Mac OS 9 at a later date. If, after you install OS X, you change your mind and decide that you want to add OS 9, you will need to do the following: First, make sure you have a Mac OS 9 or later Install CD that can boot your Mac. Next, boot the Mac from the CD, run the installer, and select the Clean Installation option. This will not harm any existing data on your hard disk.

After that, you will want to boot your hard disk under your new OS 9 installation and run the Software Update control panel in order to acquire any recent OS 9 updates. Finally, if you desire to update your Mac OS 9's version of QuickTime, you will need to run QuickTime's updater as well.

Installing OS X

When you have decided on a strategy that is best suited for your needs, you will need to back up all your data, format and partition the drive as deemed necessary, and install Mac OS 9 if needed. When those tasks are completed, you can proceed with your Mac OS X installation.

Note: From this point on, it might be helpful to sit in front of a Macintosh computer that can be used to work along with the remainder of the material covered in this book.

The Mac OS X Installation CD

To install OS X you are required to boot from the Mac OS X install CD. At this time, Mac OS X cannot be installed from a local volume, nor can it be installed from a server volume. Depending on the Macintosh, there are three ways to boot from the Mac OS X install CD. The first is by booting the Macintosh while holding down the C key. This method will work for all OS X–supported Macs. The second is by using the Startup Manager, which is only supported on NewWorld Architecture machines. Startup Manager is activated by holding down the Option key at startup. You will then be presented with a graphical interface of all available startup disk options, including NetBoot servers. The final way to boot from an OS X install CD is by inserting the CD while running either OS X or OS 9 and locating and double-clicking the Install Mac OS X application. Once you have booted the OS X install CD, the installer will automatically open, prompting you for your installation preferences.

Select Language

The OS X installer supports installations for many languages. The Select Language screen prompts you to select the appropriate language and keyboard layout for your needs. This preference can be changed at a later date, once the product is installed.

Introduction

The Introduction screen is a welcome screen that acts as a prelude to the rest of the installation process.

Read Me

The Read Me screen presents the same contents that can be found in the "Read Before You Install" document on the Mac OS X install CD.

License

The License screen presents you with OS X's Software Licensing Agreement. You must click Continue, whereupon you are presented with a second confirmation screen requesting you to click Agree before you can continue forward with the installation process.

Select Destination

The Select Destination screen allows you to choose the destination volume for your Mac OS X installation. This screen also presents you with the Erase Destination And Format As option. When installing Mac OS X on top of a preexisting installation of OS 9, do *not* select the option to erase and format the disk from within the OS X installer. This will erase the existing Mac OS 9 installation as well as all your user's applications and documents. Figure 3.1 shows the Select A Destination screen as well as the potentially disastrous Erase Destination And Format As option.

Note: According to Apple Knowledge Base Article 106442, if there is a sole ATA/ IDE hard drive in your Mac and the Select A Destination screen does not display an available hard disk to install to, you need to verify that the intended target ATA/ IDE drive is configured as a master drive on the bus.

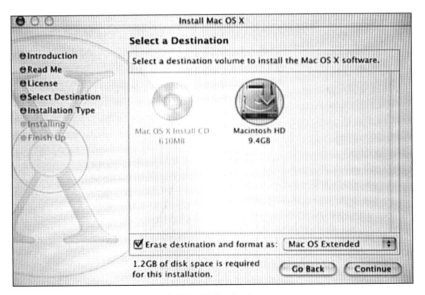

Figure 3.1   The Mac OS X installer's Select A Destination screen.

Installation Types

The Installation Types screen provides two choices for installation types. The choices are Easy Install and Custom Install. By default, the Mac OS X installer starts with Easy Install, which is composed of the options Base System Software, Essential System Software, BSD Subsystem, and Additional Print Drivers. Custom Install gives you the option of deselecting the BSD subsystem as well as the additional print drivers. Figure 3.2 depicts Mac OS X's Custom Install screen and its available options.

Note: The BSD Subsystem option is a required component for proper network functionality and network printing, whereas the Additional Print Drivers option installs drivers for Hewlett-Packard, Canon, and Epson printers.

Setup Assistant

After the software installation aspect of the Mac OS X install process has been completed, the computer will automatically reboot. Next, Mac OS X's Setup Assistant will automatically launch. The Mac Setup Assistant will then display a welcome screen that walks you through the process of product registration.

Account Information

Once you have submitted the necessary registration information, you will then need to set up your user account. Chapter 5 will review user accounts in detail,

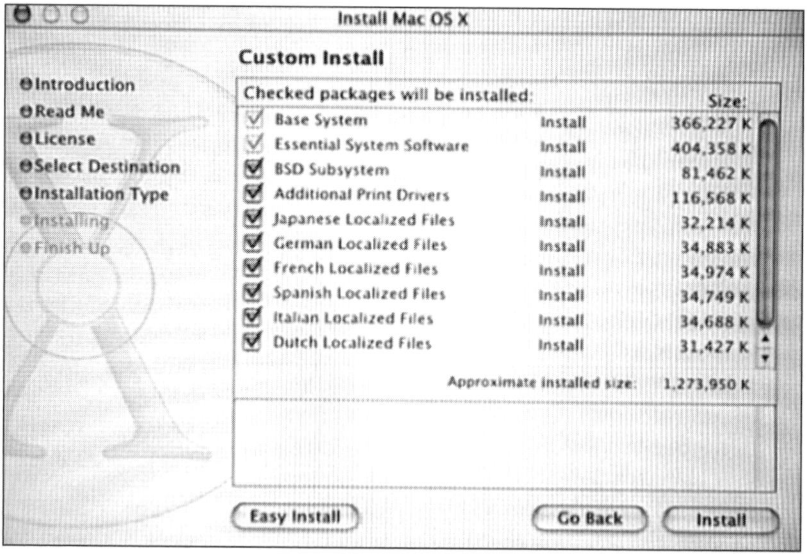

Figure 3.2   The Mac OS X installer's Custom Install screen.

but for now suffice it to say that the information you provide will be necessary to perform administrative functions within Mac OS X. When creating your local administrator account, you will need to make a *short name*, which is exactly what it sounds like—a short name. It alleviates the need for typing out your whole name.

A short name is automatically generated when you tab from the Name field to the Short Name field. But don't worry; it can be changed. A short name can have a maximum of eight characters, all lower case, and cannot contain any spaces or the following characters:

< > ' " * { } [ ] ( ) ^ ! \ # | & $? ~

Note: The only time a short name cannot be changed from the GUI is if you prematurely quit Mac OS X's Setup Assistant prior to its completion. After you have chosen your short name, you will need to provide a password. Although OS X will accept more than eight characters for this field, it only checks the first eight. Finally, the last field allows you to provide yourself an optional password hint if desired.

Get Internet Ready

The Get Internet Ready portion of the Setup Assistant provides the option to configure your Mac for Internet access. This option can only be utilized when internet connectivity is available. Figure 3.3 shows Setup Assistant's Get Internet Ready screen and its available options.

Get iTools

iTools is a set of Web-based services that Apple provides its customers. iTools services include email, Web page hosting, and Web-based file storage, to name a few. If you already possess an existing iTools account, you will be prompted to enter the appropriate user information. If you do not possess an iTools account, the Setup Assistant will allow you to create a new account. The iTools portion of the Setup Assistant is completely optional and can be bypassed by simply clicking Continue at the bottom-right corner of the screen. Figure 3.4 depicts Setup Assistant's Get iTools configuration screen.

Registration Connect

When you have satisfied the iTools registration screen, the Setup Assistant will attempt to send your registration information to Apple. If it's unsuccessful, you will be prompted to try again later.

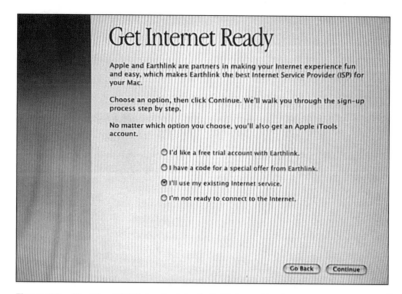

Figure 3.3 The Mac OS X Setup Assistant's Get Internet Ready screen.

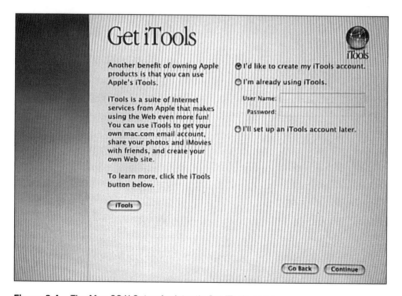

Figure 3.4 The Mac OS X Setup Assistant's Get iTools screen.

Set Up Mail

Next you will be prompted to configure an email account. By default, the Set Up Mail portion of the Setup Assistant uses your iTools account information for email client configuration. If you do not want to use iTools as your email service provider, you can manually enter the account information for an alternate email

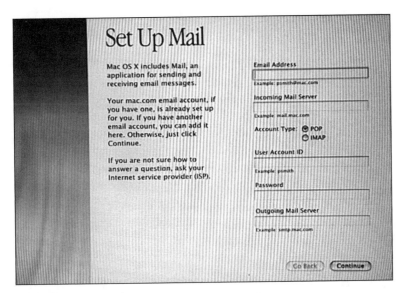

Figure 3.5   The Mac OS X Setup Assistant's Set Up Mail screen.

service, or you can skip the entire process altogether. Figure 3.5 shows Setup Assistant's Set Up Mail screen, which provides a quick and efficient way of configuring email connectivity.

Date and Time

The Date and Time portion of the Setup Assistant utilizes a Network Time Protocol (NTP) server and configures your Mac for the appropriate time zone based on your registration information. You can also manually choose a different time zone if necessary. You will now be prompted to resend your registration information if you were previously unsuccessful. At this point, the Setup Assistant will terminate, and you will be directly logged on to the desktop of OS X.

Software Update

It is important to check Apple's software downloads site for recent software updates. It is not uncommon to find that the CD in hand does not contain the most recent version of a software product. Usually, software updates can be obtained via a manufacturer's Web site. Apple simplifies this process by automating the update process upon initial OS X startup. If by some chance this does not occur, the process can be manually initiated via the Software Update preference panel. This will be reviewed in further detail in Chapter 6. Figure 3.6 shows OS X's Software Update preference panel, an excellent tool for obtaining the latest updates for Mac OS X.

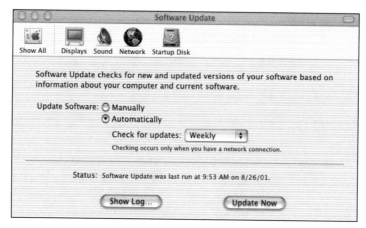

Figure 3.6 Mac OS X's Software Update preference panel.

This concludes our review of the installation process and the initial configuration of Mac OS X. As you can see, it is not a very difficult proposition to build an OS X box. Taking the time to evaluate your user's needs in applying the appropriate OS X installation strategy will go a long way toward ensuring a smooth migration from a previous Mac OS version.

Practice Questions

Question 1

> Which of the following are installation strategies for Mac OS X? [Check all correct answers]
>
> ❑ a. HFS
>
> ❑ b. Single partition
>
> ❑ c. Base system software
>
> ❑ d. Separate partitions

Answers b and d are correct. Single-partition and separate-partitions installations are Mac OS X install strategies. Answer a is incorrect because HFS, also referred to as *standard format*, is a files system that is the predecessor of HFS+, although OS X can access HFS volumes; the format is unsupported for Mac OS installation. Answer c is incorrect because Base System Software is a custom install option within the Mac OS X installer.

Question 2

> What might be a possible cause if the FTP and Telnet services are unavailable?
>
> ○ a. UFS partitioning
>
> ○ b. NewWorld Architecture
>
> ○ c. No BSD subsystem
>
> ○ d. Mac OS X only

Answer c is correct. If a Custom Install is chosen during the Mac OS X install process and the BSD Subsystem option is not selected, certain network functionality may be unavailable. Specifically, network utility, Telnet, network file system (NFS), file transfer protocol (FTP), and some network print services will not function. Answer a is incorrect because UFS partitioning is a supported format type of OS X. Answer b is incorrect because NewWorld Architecture is the name that Apple has given its hardware design for the latest generation of Macintoshes. Answer d is incorrect because "Mac OS X only" is an installation strategy for Mac OS X system.

Question 3

> What are the minimum hardware requirements for Mac OS X? [Check all
> correct answers]
>
> ❑ a. 128MB of RAM
>
> ❑ b. G4 CPU
>
> ❑ c. G3 CPU
>
> ❑ d. 1.5GB available hard disk space
>
> ❑ e. An Apple factory-supplied video card

Answers a, c, d, and e are correct. The minimum hardware requirements of Mac
OS X include an Apple factory–shipped G3 Macintosh CPU with 128MB of
RAM, an Apple-supplied video card, and 1.5GB of available hard disk space.
The only exception to this specification is the original PowerBook G3. Answer b
is incorrect because although OS X runs on a G4 processor, it is not a minimum
hardware requirement for OS X.

Question 4

> What is the name of the format best suited for most Mac OS X installs?
>
> ○ a. HFS
>
> ○ b. NTFS
>
> ○ c. HFS+
>
> ○ d. UFS

Answer c is correct. An HFS+ formatted volume will provide the most transparent
path for file migration between OS 9 and OS X. Answer a is incorrect because
HFS, also referred to as *standard format*, is a file system that is the predecessor to
HFS+. Although Mac OS X can access HFS volumes, it is not considered a desired
format for OS X installation. Answer b is incorrect because Mac OS X does not
support NTFS (Windows NT File System). Answer d is incorrect because
although supported, the UFS format has many technical disadvantages and
should be avoided. The UFS format has no advantage over the HFS+ format.

Question 5

> True or false: A Mac OS X installation is never complete unless you check
> for software updates.
>
> ○ a. True
>
> ○ b. False

Answer a is correct. Apple is constantly upgrading Mac OS X, and it cannot be
taken for granted that what is on the CD is the most current version.

Question 6

> What is it the most important task to perform before attempting any Mac OS
> X installation?
>
> ○ a. Initialize your hard disk
>
> ○ b. Run Setup Assistant
>
> ○ c. Back up all data
>
> ○ d. Obtain an iTools account

Answer c is correct. You should never attempt any major software upgrade/in-
stallation without first making a backup of all existing hard drive data.

Question 7

> True or false: Installing OS X on top of existing OS 9 data will not delete
> existing data.
>
> ○ a. True
>
> ○ b. False

Answer a is correct. Installing OS X over an existing installation will not delete
any existing data unless you select the Erase Destination And Format As option
from the Select Destination screen of the Mac OS X installer.

Need to Know More?

 For the latest OS X support developments, visit Apple's Mac OS X Support Page site located at **www.info.apple.com/usen/macosx/**.

 The Apple Knowledge Base is the definitive resource for researching Apple Technical support issues. It can be found at **http://kbase.info. apple.com/**. Check out Article ID 106472, entitled: Mac OS X FTP, SSH, and Telnet Require the BSD Subsystem

 The OS X Apple Developer site is good Web resource for additional OS X technical information. Visit it at **http://developer.apple.com/ macosx**.

Mac OS X's File System and Application Environments

Terms you'll need to understand:

- ✓ Finder
- ✓ Bundles
- ✓ Application environments
- ✓ Carbon
- ✓ Cocoa
- ✓ Packages
- ✓ Frameworks
- ✓ Java
- ✓ Path
- ✓ Pathname
- ✓ Search Path

Techniques you'll need to master:

- ✓ Understanding file locations and paths
- ✓ Comprehending the differences between aliases and symbolic links
- ✓ Knowing what a file fork is
- ✓ Recognizing file extensions
- ✓ Navigating directory organization and structure
- ✓ Identifying Library folders
- ✓ Viewing visible and hidden folders

This chapter reviews two elements of Mac OS X: The first part of this chapter will focus on Mac OS X's file system and director organization, and the second part is devoted to application environments within OS X.

Paths

From the onset, OS X was conceived to be the most Internet-centric operating system the personal computing industry had ever seen. In fact, OS X's ancestral lineage is directly tied to the creation of the World Wide Web. In 1990, Tim Berners-Lee, a researcher at the European Organization for Nuclear Research (CERN), wrote the first Web browser, called WWW (WorldWideWeb), a point-and-click (GUI) hypertext editor that ran on a Next computer.

Upon encountering OS X's directory structure, longtime Macintosh users would immediately notice that it retains some familiar elements from previous Mac OSs, such as System and Applications folders. However, unlike the old adage "the more things change, the more they stay the same," in this case, *things have changed*. Because OS X's underpinnings are based on the Berkeley Software Design (BSD) version of Unix, its file system employs many features found in Unix-based file systems.

As Macintosh operating systems go, Mac OS X has a very structured file hierarchy. When dealing with this file structure, you need to master the concept of *paths*. A path is the route to a specific file, and a pathname is the map of that path.

Note: Web browsers use paths that are referred to as URLs (Uniform Resource Locators). The URL is the path to where the data is located on the Internet. An important Mac OS X URL to know is www.apple.com/macosx.

Mac OS X File System Structure

The concept of *paths* is a central component of the OS X file system. As stated previously, Mac OS X has a very structured file hierarchy. The reason for this stems from OS X's security and resource-sharing model. Most Macintosh users are accustomed to the single-user/single-computer paradigm. They have total reign over all content on their hard disks. Mac OS 9 has a *very* limited implementation of multiple-users/single-computer sharing. It could be compared to paint on aluminum siding.

Because OS X's roots lie in the days of the Unix/monolithic computing world, it takes a completely different approach compared to what most Macintosh users are accustomed to. Mac OS X is a true multiuser operating system. When an OS X machine is shared among many users, each user *can* be provided his or her own work environment. For example, a particular work environment could contain specific applications, documents, fonts, and preferences for that particular user. When the multiple-user feature is activated within OS X, upon starting the Macintosh's, users will encounter a login screen. This is a location where users submit their username/ID and password to gain access to their specific user account. Chapter 5 reviews the different types of user privileges for system administration and access.

Note: By default, OS X is configured to automatically log in without user intervention, until otherwise specified.

We are now going to examine the contents of what the Mac OS X installer places on a hard disk. Because the Mac OS X Administration Basics exam focuses solely on OS X, we are not going to review in depth the items that the Mac OS 9 installer places on a hard disk. However, in order to remove any confusion between the two operating systems' installed items, I am going to list the Mac OS 9 items so that we can distinguish them from the OS X items. The default items that the Mac OS 9 installer places on the system include System Folder, Applications Mac OS 9, Apple Extras, and Documents. Now that we have gone over that, let's look at the Mac OS X installer's items. Use Figure 4.1 as a reference as we go over each item that the OS X installer places within the root of the hard disk.

System

Just like OS 9, OS X has a System folder. Unlike OS 9's folder, which is named System Folder, Mac OS X's folder is named just System. Both System folders contain critical system resources, but, unlike in OS 9, most users do not have access to make modifications or add more resources. This protects Mac OS X from less adroit users, allowing the system to remain untarnished, which translates to an overall system stability gain.

Library Folders

Library folders are a new addition to the Mac OS. A Library folder contains user-customizable resources and preferences. Some examples of the contents that can be found in a Library folder are fonts, desktop pictures, alert sounds, modem scripts, printer drivers, and application preferences. In fact, there are many Library folders. In preparation for the exam, you will specifically need to know about two kinds of Library folders.

Figure 4.1   The OS X folder structure within the root of the hard disk.

The first type of Library folder is the one that can be found at the root of the hard disk. This is the folder that contains system-wide customizable resources and preferences. The contents of this particular Library folder can only be altered by a system administrator. We will cover system administrators as well as other types of user accounts in Chapter 5.

The second type of Library folder you will encounter is a user's Library folder. If you are utilizing Mac OS X's multiple-users feature, you will encounter a Library folder in each user's home folder. The user Library folders contain user-specific customizable resources and preferences. This leads us to our next item of review: users' home folders.

Users' Home Folders

Another folder that is installed on the volume by default is the Users folder. When Mac OS X's multiple-users feature is utilized, each user account is provided its own home folder. Let's say, for example, that a particular OS X system you administer has four users—Sam, Frank, Tammi, and David. If you look inside the Users folder (Figure 4.2), you will see individual folders created for each of these users, plus one folder called the Shared folder. There will be one folder for Sam, one folder for Frank, one folder for Tammi, and one for David.

*Note: The folder that is represented with a **house icon** denotes the home directory for the current logged-in user.*

Within the Frank, Tammi, and David folders, you will find that they each contain an identical structure of subfolders. Figure 4.3 depicts these folders, which include Desktop, Documents, Library, Movies, Music, Pictures, Public, and Sites.

 The command-line jargon for a home folder for a currently logged-in user is "~/". The ~ symbol is a "tilde," pronounced *til-da*.

Desktop
The Desktop folder contains any items located on the desktop for the particular user.

Documents
The Documents folder is, by default, the location for the particular user's accounts and documents, such as Word, Excel, and PowerPoint.

Library
The user's Library folder, as mentioned earlier, contains user-specific customizable resources and preferences for the particular user.

Figure 4.2   A peek inside the Users folder.

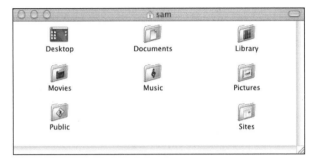

Figure 4.3   The folder structure within a user's folder.

Movies, Music, and Pictures

Because the Macintosh is marketed as the "Digital Hub," Apple conveniently creates individual folders for movies, music, and pictures within every user's home folder. The idea is that digital content is to be stored within the appropriate folder. MP3 files go in Music, QuickTime files go in Movies, and Pic files (pictures) go in Pictures.

Public

The Public folder is the location of contents to be shared over a network. Unlike previous Macintosh operating systems, Mac OS X has been designed with a predesignated share point. The predesignated share point restricts network access to one folder, thus providing additional control as to what can be accessed through network file sharing.

Sites

The Sites folder is the default directory for Web pages that are to be shared with Mac OS X's built-in Apache Web server. Apache is a Unix-based "Open Source" Web server that is freely distributed. It is considered to be, by far, the most deployed Web server on the planet.

Shared Folder

Each user account has its own login. When one user account is logged in, it can only see the contents of its own Users folder. It cannot see the contents of other user's home folders. For example, if user Frank is logged in, he cannot see the contents of Tammi's Users folder, and vice versa. This brings us back to that one straggler folder within the Users home folder—the Shared folder. The Shared folder is the place where local user accounts can share files among themselves locally on the system. Although files can be copied or saved into the Shared folder, once they are there they cannot be modified. Instead, they must be copied out to a folder that the current user has permission to modify. Only the owner of the original file can modify it once it is placed in the Shared folder.

Applications Folder

The Applications folder contains all user-accessible software programs. These programs can include productivity applications, games, and utilities (which has its own subfolder).

Invisible Items

Just like Mac OS 9, Mac OS X's file system contains invisible items. These invisible items can include both files and folders. Although normal users and administrators will be unable to modify invisible items, they can be listed via the Go To Folder command under the Go menu in the Finder, shown in Figure 4.4, or through the Terminal application within the Utilities folder.

Aliases and Symbolic Links

Aliases and symbolic links are files that contain the pathnames to other files or folders. Aliases and symbolic links lead/connect you to other files or folders. I always use a telephone number analogy when I try to teach the concept of aliases to end users. Aliases are like mobile phones in the sense that, if you want to contact a specific person, and you knew that this person can be reached via a mobile phone, then the phone number is the "alias" for that specific person. The mobile phone number would be the file/representation containing the pathname that leads you to contacting that specific person through the phone network.

I use a mobile phone for my alias analogy because symbolic links work slightly different. An alias works like a mobile phone in the sense that no matter where a specific file or folder resides, the alias can locate and connect to it. For the most part, an alias can dynamically locate its specific target file or folder, even if you move that file or folder to a different location within the same volume. On the other hand, a symbolic link is more akin to a land line, in the sense that it con-

Figure 4.4 The Go To Folder command.

tains exact information as to where a file or folder resides. Therefore, if you move a file or folder that the symbolic link references to a different location, the symbolic link breaks. An alias is a reference/link to a specific file, whereas a symbolic link places more emphasis on the path/location of a specified file. This means that if a symbolic link's target file is replaced in the same exact location with a new file, it still references that file. On a day-to-day basis, you will only be dealing with aliases. For the most part, you should not encounter symbolic links. They are concealed within the underpinnings of Mac OS X.

Search Paths

Just like OS 9, Mac OS X has a Finder. As with previous Macintosh multi-Finder operating systems, its function remains the same. The Finder is the mechanism that facilitates user file access within the Macintosh operating system. Because OS X contains many different locations for its customizable resources and preferences, it is important to understand the concept of *search paths* within the Finder. A search path is an ordered search for resources within a Mac OS X system. For instance, Mac OS X looks for installed fonts in five locations. The location where the fonts reside determines who has access to them. Table 4.1 illustrates the order in which OS X searches for its available fonts. Chapter 6 contains more in-depth coverage of font management.

Table 4.1 The search path for fonts.	
Search Path	**Location**
~/Library/Fonts	The Fonts folder inside the Library folder inside the user's home folder
/ Library/Fonts	The Fonts folder inside the Library folder inside the root of the volume
/Network/Library/Fonts	The Fonts folder inside the Library folder on the network
/System/Library/fonts	The Fonts folder inside the Library folder inside the System folder
Mac OS 9 Fonts folder	Dependent on whether Mac OS 9 is installed and where it resides on the volume

Note: As a general rule of thumb, most search paths work their way from the user's home folder to the System folder, as illustrated in Table 4.1. Also, an example of how Mac OS X manages who has access to what files is this: Fonts that are located within a specific user's home folder are only accessible to that specific user.

File Forks and Extensions

Traditionally, desktop Macintosh operating systems have employed a technology referred to as *file forks*. In Mac OS 9 and previous Mac operating systems, a file is comprised of two parts: a data fork and a resource fork. The data fork is the actual file itself. The resource fork is composed of metadata, which is descriptive information about data. In this instance, the metadata that is contained within the resource fork describes the file type/application association and icon information. The resource fork allows the file to be opened with its appropriate parent application by being double-clicked. The one inherent problem with resource forks is that their functionality is limited to Macintosh operating systems only. Resource forks do not transfer to other non-Macintosh operating systems without the utilization of third-party compatibility software. Files that cannot find their parent applications are referred to as *orphaned*.

Mac OS X retains the functionality of resource forks, but it provides for an additional built-in mechanism of cross-platform compatibility—file extensions. A file extension is a designation included in the name of a file in order to help associate it with its appropriate parent application. Some examples of file extensions are .pdf, .doc, .jpg, .tiff, and .html. A PDF readme document might look like this: README.pdf. File extensions allow OS X to be a good citizen in the network file-sharing world, especially with Microsoft operating system products.

Mac OS X's Application Environments

The final part in this chapter deals with application environments. Application environments allow Mac OS X to run its modern OS-enabled applications while simultaneously supporting legacy Mac OS software. In Chapter 2, we briefly touched on Classic. Although I referred to Classic as a compatibility environment for running legacy Macintosh software, it is known as an *application environment*. An application environment consists of various system resources, components, and services that allow an application to function under OS X. Mac OS X has five application environments: Cocoa, Carbon, Java, BSD, and Classic.

Note: Classic will be reviewed in detail in Chapter 8.

Cocoa

Cocoa applications are specifically developed for Mac OS X. Cocoa applications are incompatible with older Macintosh operating systems and therefore will not run on Mac OS 9. Cocoa applications take advantage of all of Mac OS X's modern OS features, such as advance memory management, preemptive multitasking, symmetric multiprocessing, and the Aqua interface. Some examples of Cocoa applications are OS X's Mail and Preview applications as well as Netopia's Timbuktu for Mac OS X.

Carbon

The greatest advantage of the Carbon application environment is that developers can build applications that run in either Mac OS 9 or OS X. When running within OS X, Carbon applications take advantage of most of Mac OS X's modern OS features, including the Aqua interface. In order for Carbon applications to run within Mac OS 9, the CarbonLib library must be present within the Extensions folder within the Mac OS 9 System Folder. Some examples of Carbon applications are AppleWorks 6.1, Acrobat Reader 5.0, and Quicken 2001.

Packages and Bundles

A package, sometimes referred to as a *bundle*, is a single icon point-and-click representation of an application. Just like previous Classic applications, Mac OS X's Carbon and Cocoa applications can be composed of multiple subordinate files and resources. In the GUI, all these subordinate pieces are neatly wrapped up into a representation of a single executable file for the end user. To view the contents of an application package, simply hold down the Control key while highlighting the Carbon or Cocoa application icon. You are then given the option to show the package's contents. For illustration purposes, Figure 4.5 depicts the contents of Internet Explorer for Mac OS X.

Frameworks

Mac OS X frameworks are analogous to Mac OS 9 shared libraries in that they both contain dynamically loading code that is shared by multiple applications. Frameworks alleviate the need for applications that contain common code to load that code multiple times while running simultaneously. Mac OS 9's shared libraries can be found within the Extensions folder inside the System Folder. Examples of shared libraries are Applescript and CarbonLib.

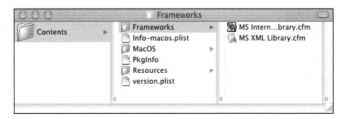

Figure 4.5 Internet Explorer's package contents.

Java

The Mac OS X Java environment is 100-percent Java 2 Standard Edition compliant. It can run both Java applications and applets. The key advantage of Java development is that Java applications can run on any platform that contains a cross-compatible Java Virtual Machine.

BSD

The BSD application environment usually deals with command-line executable shell scripts. A shell script is similar to an MS-DOS batch file in that they are both text files that contain a sequence of commands. Interestingly enough, shell scripts do not necessarily have to be executed from the command line. Shell scripts can be implemented within Cocoa applications, thus allowing them to be executed from the GUI.

This is the last chapter in this book to solely focus on the conceptual material that will be required for the Mac OS X Administration Basics exam. From here on, the text of this book will focus more on the "how to" knowledge that is required to administer Mac OS X. To achieve the highest level of exam success, try to maintain a good balance between the practical and the theoretical know-how.

Practice Questions

Question 1

What is the name of the order in which OS X acquires its resources?

○ a. Library

○ b. Symbolic links

○ c. Go To Folder command

○ d. Search path

Answer d is correct. A search path is an ordered search for resources within a Mac OS X system. Answer a is incorrect because the Library folder contains user-customizable resources and preferences. Answer b is incorrect because symbolic links are files that contain the pathnames to other files or folders. Answer c is incorrect because the Go To Folder command within the Finder allows the user to navigate to a specific item by specifying a path.

Question 2

Which of the following is an OS X application environment?

○ a. Java

○ b. Cocoa

○ c. BSD

○ d. Carbon

○ e. All of the above

Answer e is correct. In addition to all the listed items, Classic is also an application environment of OS X.

Question 3

What is Mac OS X's equivalent to Mac OS 9's shared libraries?

○ a. Package

○ b. Bundle

○ c. Microkernal

○ d. Library

○ e. None of the above

Answer e is correct. Frameworks are Mac OS X's equivalent to Mac OS 9's shared libraries. Answer a is incorrect; a package is a series of files that comprise the underpinnings of a specific application and are represented by a single icon within the Finder. Answer b is incorrect; the term *bundle* is synonymous with a package. Answer c is incorrect; the microkernal is OS X's foundation that provides basic services for all other parts of the operating system. Answer d is incorrect because a Library folder contains user-customizable resources and preferences.

Question 4

True or false: Mac OS X is not a true multiuser operating system.

○ a. True

○ b. False

Answer b is correct. Mac OS X *is* a true multiuser operating system.

Question 5

What is another name for packages?

○ a. Frameworks

○ b. Libraries

○ c. Bundles

○ d. TIFF

Answer c is correct. Packages are sometimes referred to as *bundles*. Answer a is incorrect; an OS X framework is analogous to a Mac OS 9 shared library in that it is dynamically loading code that is shared by multiple applications. Answer b is incorrect because, as a rule of thumb, the Library folder contains user-customizable resources and preferences. Answer d is incorrect; a TIFF (Tagged Image File Format) is a type of graphics file.

Question 6

A file that contains pathnames to other files or folders is called what? [Check all correct answers]

❏ a. Search path

❏ b. Symbolic link

❏ c. Alias

❏ d. Framework

Answers b and c are correct. Aliases and symbolic links are files that contain the pathnames to other files or folders. Answer a is incorrect because a search path is an ordered search for resources within a Mac OS X system. Answer d is incorrect because an OS X framework is dynamically loading code that is shared by multiple applications.

Question 7

> What are some of the folders a typical user's home folder might contain?
> [Check all correct answers]
>
> ❑ a. Sites
>
> ❑ b. Desktop
>
> ❑ c. System
>
> ❑ d. Library
>
> ❑ e. None of the above

Answers a, b, and d are correct. A user's home folder will always contain Sites, Desktop, and Library folders. Answer c is incorrect because the System folder resides in the root of the Mac OS X startup volume. Answer e is incorrect due to the inclusion of answers a, b, and d.

Need to Know More?

 The Apple Knowledge Base is the definitive resource for researching Apple Technical support issues. It can be found at **http://kbase.info. apple.com/**.

Check out Article ID 106419, entitled: Mac OS X: About Folders, Directories and Path Names.

 For the latest Carbon and Cocoa applications, visit Apple's Mac OS X Downloads page at **www.apple.com/downloads/macosx/**.

Users and Privileges

Terms you'll need to understand:

✓ Root

✓ Administrator

✓ Normal user

✓ Groups

✓ Permissions

Techniques you'll need to master:

✓ Identifying types of users

✓ Creating and deleting user accounts via the Users preferences pane

✓ Administrating the Mac OS X Login

✓ Understanding and managing privileges

This chapter focuses solely on how Mac OS X deals with users and privileges. As stated in the previous chapter, Mac OS X is Apple's first true multiuser desktop operating system. Because of Mac OS X's Unix underpinnings, it has the ability to employ a Unix-style security model. In OS X, each user is provided with his or her own user account. Each user account provides a separate customizable workspace/environment for its assigned user.

Identifying Types of Users

All user accounts are assigned a series of attributes. These attributes include a long name, short name, password, and UID (User ID). A UID is a behind-the-scenes mechanism that OS X employs to identify users by unique numeric designations. Three types of user accounts can be configured within OS X: root, administrator, and normal user.

Root

In UNIX, the root account, which is sometimes referred to as the *system administrator* or the *superuser account*, has complete access to all settings and files within the operating system. When logged in via the root account, you are master of all that is within Mac OS X. Generally, the root account is used for the express purposes of system administration. Administration via the root account is something to grow into. As useful as the root account may be for administering an OS X system, for the less-skillful user there is an equal chance of really messing things up. Therefore, if you are unsure of exactly what you are doing, do *not* use the root account.

You don't need to create a root user account. OS X systems have a root account, but it is disabled by default. Apple intentionally designed Mac OS X in this fashion to prevent less-adroit users from breaking the OS. In order to gain access to the root account, you must first enable it. This is can be done via the NetInfo Manager, which will be covered in Chapter 6. In fact, all user accounts can be administered through the NetInfo Manager utility, although this is beyond the scope of the material covered in this book. If you are curious to learn more about the NetInfo Manager utility, check out the "Need to Know More?" section at the end of this chapter.

Administrator (Admin)

For day-to-day system administration, the admin user account is where it's at. The admin account has enough power to get the majority of the system administration tasks done without the potential liabilities associated with the root account. An admin user account provides access to all of Mac OS X's system preferences and utilities, and it provides the ability to install applications and system-wide resources. An admin account also has the ability to create and manage other user accounts within an OS X system.

As mentioned in Chapter 3, the Mac OS X Installation Setup Assistant walks you through the initial configuration of the first administrator account. Within Mac OS X, there can be multiple admin accounts per OS X system. This is a useful feature in the event that one admin forgets his password and requires a password reset, which can only be accomplished by another accessible admin user account.

Normal User

A normal user is your typical end user. A normal user account does not allow system-wide administration of Mac OS X. In fact, if a normal user attempts to install software, he or she would be confronted by a screen with a padlock that requires an administrator's authorization before any installation can commence. A normal user account cannot modify system-wide preferences. These include Date & Time, Energy Saver, Login (Window), Network, Startup Disk, and Users. A normal user typically has the ability to modify any other preference that pertains to his own user account

Note: Chapter 6 will further review Mac OS X's system preferences.

Groups

Typically within the Unix security model, groups are used to simplify the assignment of system access to a series of users intended to share the same level of system access. There are three preset groups within Mac OS X: admin, staff, and wheel. Mac OS X atomically handles the assignment of groups. The group staff is the standard group all user accounts are assigned to. Admin users are also members of the admin and wheel groups. The admin and wheel groups have access to make system-wide changes. Just as users are assigned unique numerical user IDs, all groups have unique numerical IDs as well. Mac OS X does not provide an easy-to-use GUI for managing groups, although they can be managed through the NetInfo Manager as well as via the command line.

Managing Accounts Via the Users Preferences Pane

Within Mac OS X's GUI, the most day-to-day user account administration is done through the Users preferences pane. The Users preferences pane can configure both admin and normal user accounts; it is also the location where you delete accounts and change account passwords. The root account does not appear within the Users preferences pane. As stated previously, the root account already exists, but in order to gain access to it, you will need to enable it through the NetInfo Manager, which is covered in Chapter 6. Figure 5.1 shows the Users preferences pane.

When opening the Users preferences pane for the first time, you will notice that one admin account is already created. This is the admin account that is generated by the Setup Assistant during the Mac OS X install process. By default, Mac OS X is configured to automatically log in utilizing this admin account. Once an additional user account is created, you are queried as to whether you want to turn off automatic login. If automatic login is disabled, on the next restart you will be presented with a list of user accounts to choose from for logging in. Figure 5.2 shows the Login window with a list of user accounts.

As previously stated, you can have more than one admin account on the same machine. Conversely, you can delete an admin account, but you will be prevented from deleting all admin accounts. Every OS X system must have at least one admin account at all times.

When you create a new particular account, you also simultaneously create a home directory folder for that user, as discussed in Chapter 4. However, when you delete a user account, you do not delete that user's home directory. Rather, you are prompted to transfer ownership of that directory to an existing admin user account. The deleted user's home folder will have its name changed from "user" to "user deleted." If by chance you change your mind and decide to reinstate a deleted user account, you must first re-create the user's account from scratch. Next, using the account that was assigned ownership of the deleted user's data, manually drag the contents from the deleted user's folder into the new user's folder. Figure 5.3 shows a deleted user's deleted home folder as well as her re-instated/newly created user folder.

Note: Although this knowledge is not required for the examination, you have three ways in which you can remove a deleted user's home directory from a Mac OS X system. The first way is to remove the deleted user's home directory by booting into Mac OS 9 and simply trashing the desired folder. The second way is to remove the deleted user's home directory by utilizing the root user account and simply trashing the folder via the GUI. The third and final way, however, is the official Apple method, as outlined in AppleCare Knowledge Base Article ID 106256, which basically tells you how to remove the folder via the Terminal application utilizing the sudo (superuser do, which is covered in Chapter 9) command. This method circumvents the liabilities of the root user account, and you avoid having to use that old Mac 9 OS stuff.

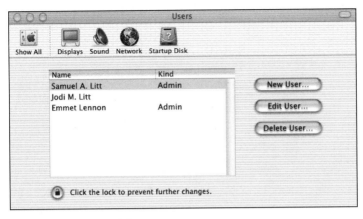

Figure 5.1   The Users preferences pane.

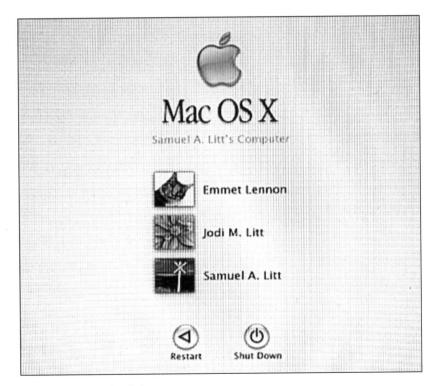

Figure 5.2   The Login window.

Privileges/Permissions

Central to Mac OS X's multiuser security model is the concept of *privileges*. Simply stated, privileges (which Unix folk refer to as *permissions*) provide the control mechanism for access to files, folders, and applications within Mac OS X. In Mac OS 9, privileges composed the security component of network file sharing. In Mac OS X,

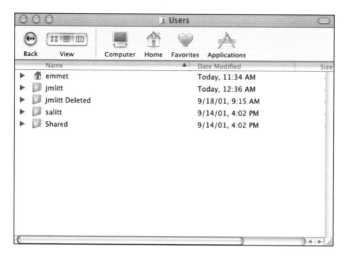

Figure 5.3 An accidental deletion of a user account does not translate into data loss. The deleted user's data still exists. If you decide to reinstate the user account, you will need to transfer the data from her (deleted) user account folder—especially if the user account is your wife's.

privileges/permissions retain their network file sharing security role, while expanding its functionality to include security for local system data. Because Mac OS X was designed for a single computer to be shared among many users, it necessitated developing a means to prevent one user's data from being accessed or deleted by another user. This is where privileges/permissions come into play. In an OS X system, every file, folder, and application—basically anything that can be accessed—is assigned a user and a set of privileges/permissions. Mac OS X has three basic levels of privileges: read, write, and execute.

Read

The read privilege allows users to see and copy the contents of files and folders. The read privilege does not allow for the deletion or modification of those contents.

Write

The write privilege allows users to modify the contents of files and folders. The write privilege allows for the deletion of as well as the addition to those contents.

Execute

The execute privilege allows users to run applications and view the contents of a folder. Within Mac OS X's GUI, the execute privileges are managed behind the scenes without user intervention. When an item is assigned read access, it is automatically assigned execute access as well. For all intents and purposes, an item assigned an execute privilege other than a folder appears to OS X as an application. Execute privileges can be manually assigned via the command line, although you will not need to know how to do this for the exam.

Setting Privileges Using the Info Window

Within OS X's GUI, privileges are set via the item's Info window. This is done by selecting the item within the Finder and choosing the Show Info command under the File menu or by utilizing the key combination Command+I and choosing Show Privileges. The GUI tries to simplify the assignment of privileges by grouping them into four choices: Read Only, Write Only, Read & Write, and None. Although folders can be assigned any of the specified privileges, files can only be assigned Read Only, Read & Write, or None. When a folder is assigned Write Only, that folder becomes a shared "drop box" for users other than its owner.

There are three categories for privilege assignment: user (owner), group, and other (everyone). The owner category is the user account that initially created or installed the particular file, folder, or application being inspected. By default, the group that is listed within the Info window is "staff." Mac OS X does not provision any means of changing group assignment through the GUI. Groups play a greater role within Mac OS X Server. Lastly, the everyone category assigns privileges for everyone not listed within the owner and group categories. Figure 5.4 depicts the Privileges portion of the Info window. As a side note, a couple of shareware applications are available that provide the enhanced functionality of a Mac OS X's standard Show Info window. They are Super Get Info by Bare Bones software and Get Info by Gideon Softworks. Both of these utilities do pretty much the same thing—either one can be obtained through the Mac OS X section of VersionTracker's Web site, using the URL **www.versiontracker.com/macosx/index.shtml**.

Here are some quick and important tips regarding the assignment of privileges:

➤ Mac OS 9 does not respect the Mac OS X's security model. If an OS X system is rebooted into OS 9, the entire contents of the system are exposed to viewing, modification, and deletion.

➤ The movement of files, folders, and applications within an OS X system does not modify privileges.

➤ Files do not automatically inherit the privileges of the folder they reside in.

➤ Even if you have not been assigned access to a particular file, you can still delete it if you have read and write access to the folder it resides in.

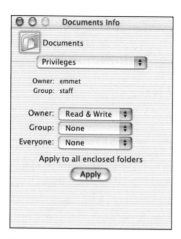

Figure 5.4 The Privileges portion of a typical Info window.

➤ Depending on your expectations of data security, when using external media such as removable media and hard disks, you may need to review and assign appropriate privileges in order to protect and facilitate the access data.

➤ Locally mounted volumes within Mac OS X can be configured to ignore privileges. When enabled, this will remove file security, allowing all contents to be accessed by whatever user is logged in. This feature is enabled by checking the Ignore Privileges On This Volume option in the Info window of the intended partition. A word of caution: Up until OS X (10.1), a user could enable this feature for the startup volume when logged in using an admin account with little consequence. Since version 10.1, this feature can only be enabled through the root user account. I can tell you from personal experience that if Ignore Privileges On This Volume is enabled on the startup partition, components of Mac OS X will cease to function properly. My advice: Do *not* use this feature on your startup partition.

How to Read Permissions and Ownership from the Command Line

Last but not least, it is important that you know how to interpret permissions and ownership rights when viewing the contents of the hard disk using the command line. The exam does contain material that will require you to know this. For Figure 5.5, I used the "ll" (long list directory contents) command within the Terminal application.

One of the most important concepts to master when working with Mac OS X is knowing that, regardless of whether you are using the GUI or using the command line, you are using the same OS. Privilege and ownership changes that are

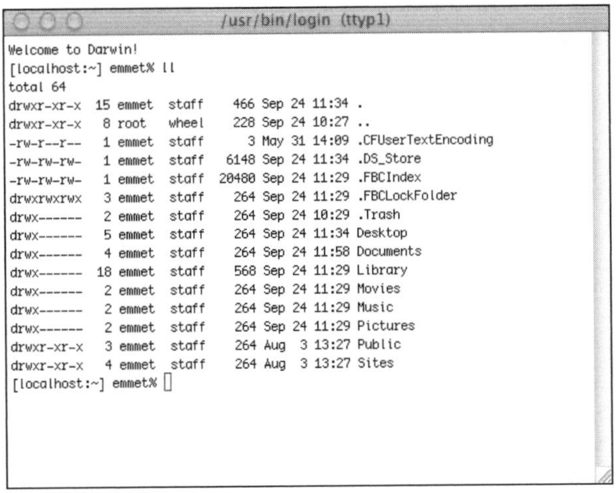

Figure 5.5 The privleges for Emmet's home directory as displayed within the Terminal application using the "ll" command.

made using the GUI's Info window will appear in the command line, and vice versa. To illustrate this point, refer to Figure 5.6.

Here's the breakdown of the designations for Figure 5.6:

➤ A is the item type: a hyphen (-) for regular files, lowercase letter *d* for directories, and a lowercase letter *l* for symbolic links.

➤ B depicts the item's privileges/permissions. This is further broken down as follows: 1 represents the user's (owner's) permissions, 2 represents the specified group's permissions, and 3 represents permissions for other (everyone else). As discussed earlier, directory items have three basic levels of designation: read, write, and execute. These are represented by *r* for read, *w* for write, and *x* for execute.

➤ C is the item's link count. A *link count* indicates the number of directory entries that refer to the same file. You will not need to know this for the test.

➤ D is the item's user (owner).

➤ E is the item's specified group.

➤ F is the item's file size.

➤ G is the item's last date of modification.

➤ H is the item's last time of modification.

➤ I is the item's name.

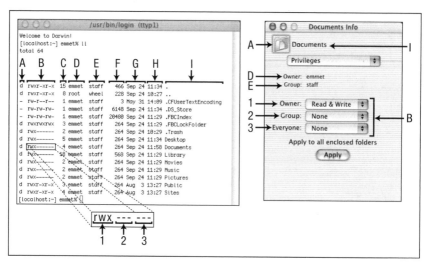

Figure 5.6 This figure is composed of two parts. The left side of the figure depicts a terminal window listing the contents of a user's home directory. In this instance, the user is Emmet. The right side contains a Show Info window depicting the permissions for Emmet's Documents folder. I have broken down the contents of the terminal window into columns, each with an assigned letter.

In Figure 5.6, you will notice that there are corresponding labels in both the Terminal window and the Info window portions of the figure. The corresponding labels are as follows: A, B, D, E, I, 1, 2, and 3. These labels represent the corresponding item attributes that can be viewed and administered by both the GUI and the Terminal application within Mac OS X.

When looking at the Terminal window portion of the figure, pay special attention to column B for the documents item. You will notice that the permissions are as follows: owner rwx (read, write, execute); group, none; and everyone, none. Now upon examining the Show Info window portion of the figure, you will notice that the owner has Read & Write privileges, the group has none, and everyone has none. The only thing missing from the Show Info window is the depiction of execute privileges. There is no need for manual assignment of execute privileges because this is handled automatically within the OS. Folders within Mac OS X are always given execute privileges.

As you can see, both the Terminal window and the Show Info window for the documents folder are depicting identical item privileges. You will also notice that labels A, D, E, I, 1, 2, and 3 also depict identical item attributes in both the Terminal window and the Show Info window for the documents folder. That is because, as previously stated, regardless of whether you choose to use the Mac OS X's GUI or the command line, you are still using the same operating system.

Although this chapter does not have a broad range of topicality, it does cover some of the most important and difficult concepts for the administration of Mac OS X. Even though you may already be familiar with the concepts of privileges and permissions from other operating systems, I recommend that you take some extra time in reviewing this chapter's material due to its significance.

Practice Questions

Question 1

> Within Mac OS X, system-wide changes can be administered from which of
> the following accounts? [Check all correct answers]
>
> ❏ a. System administrator
>
> ❏ b. Administrator
>
> ❏ c. Normal user
>
> ❏ d. None of the above

Answers a and b are correct. The system administrator account and an administrator account can both make system-wide changes within Mac OS X. The system administrator account is also known as the *root* or *superuser* account. Answer
c is incorrect because a normal user is incapable of making system-wide changes.
Answer d is incorrect because answers a and b are correct.

Question 2

> True or false: Mac OS X is a true multiuser desktop operating system.
>
> ○ a. True
>
> ○ b. False

Answer a is correct. Mac OS X is Apple's first true multiuser operating system.

Question 3

What can you tell from the following set of permissions?

`rwxr-xr-x`

○ a. Everyone has read, write, and execute privileges for this item.

○ b. No one has access to this item.

○ c. The group has read and write privileges for this item.

○ d. The user has read, write, and execute privileges for this item.

Answer d is correct. The user has read, write, and execute privileges for this item. As for the other privileges, the group has read and execute privileges as well as everyone else. Therefore, answers a, b, and c are incorrect.

Question 4

True or false: Execute privileges can manually be administered through the command line.

○ a. True

○ b. False

Answer a is correct. True execute privileges can be manually administered through the command line.

Question 5

> User accounts can be administered via which of the following? [Check all correct answers]
>
> ❏ a. Login window
>
> ❏ b. Users preference pane
>
> ❏ c. Command line
>
> ❏ d. NetInfo Manager
>
> ❏ e. All of the above

Answers b, c, and d are correct. User accounts can be administered via the Users preference pane, the command line, and the NetInfo Manager. Answer a is incorrect because the Login window cannot be used to administer user accounts. Answer e is incorrect because only answers b, c, and d are correct.

Question 6

> True or false: An admin user account can have its password reset by another admin user.
>
> ○ a. True
>
> ○ b. False

Answer a is correct. In the event that an admin user forgets his or her password, another admin user can reset it.

Question 7

> True or false: A file can be deleted by a user who has not been assigned rwx access privileges to that file.
>
> ○ a. True
>
> ○ b. False

Answer a is correct. Even if a user has not been assigned *any* access privileges to a particular file, he can still delete it if he has read and write access to the folder the file resides in.

Question 8

What are the attributes of a user account? [Check all correct answers]

❏ a. Login

❏ b. UID

❏ c. Long name

❏ d. Short name

❏ e. All of the above

Answers b, c, and d are correct. A long name, short name, password, and UID (User ID) are all attributes of a user account. Answer a is incorrect because a login is not a user account attribute. Answer e is incorrect because only answers b, c, and d are correct.

Question 9

What does UID stand for?

○ a. Unique Identification Designation

○ b. Unique ID

○ c. User ID

○ d. None of the above

Answer c is correct. UID stands for User ID, which is a unique number that Mac OS X assigns a user account for identification purposes. Therefore, answers a, b, and d are incorrect.

Question 10

True or false: When an OS X system is booted back into OS 9, Mac OS X's security model is preserved.

○ a. True

○ b. False

Answer b is correct. Mac OS 9 does not preserve Mac OS X's security model. If an OS X system is rebooted into OS 9, the entire contents of the system are exposed to viewing, modification, and deletion.

Need to Know More?

 Check out Article ID 1067 on the AppleCare Knowledge Base site by going to **http://kbase.info.apple.com/cgi-bin/WebObjects/kbase. woa/wa/query?type=ids&val=106428&x=77&y=15@**.

 Download the "Understanding and Using NetInfo" manual from Apple's Manuals section on the support site. You will need Adobe Acrobat Reader to view the manual. Although it is not required reading for the exam, this manual is Apple's definitive guide to the NetInfo Manager application. The URL for this document is **www.info.apple. com/info.apple.com/manuals/manuals.taf?search=Description& string=netinfo&manlang=en&start=1&lang=&geo=**.

Administration and Resources

Terms you'll need to understand:

✓ System preferences
✓ Pane
✓ Search path
✓ Directory service

Techniques you'll need to master:

✓ Administering the Mac OS X's System Preferences application
✓ Configuring languages
✓ Setting up Login items
✓ Selecting a directory service
✓ Enabling the root user account
✓ Configuring a printer via the Print Center
✓ Implementing FireWire and USB peripherals
✓ Managing fonts

This chapter begins the transition into the practical knowledge required to pass the Mac OS X Administration Basics exam. As with all computer desktop support knowledge, it is important to have a balance between theoretical and applicable knowledge—and Mac OS X is no exception. The exam will require a demonstration of both, but it will not require you to be the quintessential expert in either. Rather, the exam will focus on specific topicality that Apple has deemed most important to know. You will not need to recite the AppleCare Knowledge Base verbatim, although you should consider it a "useful tool" in your quest to achieve a passing grade on the exam. This chapter will focus on key aspects of Mac OS X system administration "know-how" that the exam will require you to demonstrate.

The System Preferences Application

Within Mac OS 9, system software and settings are configured through a series of small programs known as Control Panel Devices (CDEVs). Within Mac OS X, system software configuration and settings are managed via a central program known as the System Preferences application. Although the administration of system preferences is now handled through a single point, they are still analogous to Mac OS 9's CDEVs in the sense that they are really a series of smaller packages/bundles managed through the System Preferences application.

Configuration of system settings within the System Preferences application is done through a Quartz GUI element known as a *pane*. When a specific system preference is selected, the corresponding preference pane is loaded within the System Preferences application. Preference panes redraw themselves within the confines of the initial System Preferences application window. The System Preferences window has a fixed width, but it will resize itself vertically as necessary to accommodate the contents of the preference pane being viewed.

The contents of the System Preferences application are divided up into five divisions/categories: Personal, Hardware, Internet & Network, System, and a user customizable area. The Personal section contains the preferences for Desktop, Dock, General, International, Login, Screen Saver and Universal Access. Through the Hardware section, the ColorSync, Displays, Energy Saver, Keyboard, Mouse and Sound preferences can be configured. Within the Internet and Network section, the Internet, Network, QuickTime, and Sharing preferences can be configured. The System section contains the Classic, Date & Time, Software Update, Speech, Startup Disk, and Users preferences.

Finally, there is the user customizable section, which resides at the top of the System Preferences application screen. This section contains user-selected System Preferences pane shortcuts that can be accessed from any point within the

System Preference application. By default, the following System Preferences pane shortcuts reside in this section: Displays, Sound, Network, and Startup Disk. Any of the default system preference shortcuts can be deleted, as desired. Also, any of the preferences within the System Preferences application can have short-cuts in the user-customizable section. Figure 6.1 reveals the System Preferences application in all its glory.

As for the system preferences, this book does not cover all of them in depth. Most of the critical information necessary for the administration of the system preferences can be garnered from just playing around with the System Prefer-ences application. If you need a written reference on the configuration of system preferences, you'll be glad to know that many books are available on the topic. In fact, The Coriolis Group publishes two such books: *The Mac OS X Book: The Ultimate Macintosh User's Guide*, by Mark R. Bell, and *Mac OS X Little Black Book*, by Gene Steinberg. Both of these titles will suffice quite nicely. However, this study guide will only hone in on five specific preferences within the System Preferences application: International, Login, Network, Sharing, and Classic. This chapter covers the administration of the Language tab within the International and Login preference panes. Chapter 7 is entirely devoted to the configuration of the Network and Sharing preference panes, whereas the administration of the Classic preference pane is covered in Chapter 8. These five preference panes have

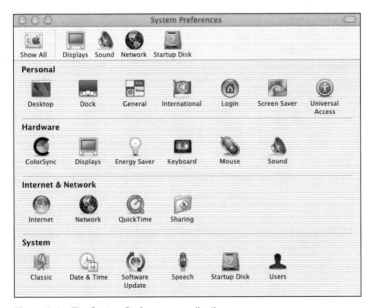

Figure 6.1 The System Preferences application.

been selected because they are the most extensively tested ones on the exam. Besides, how many questions could be asked about screen savers and mouse configuration anyway?

Configuring Languages

Mac OS X has two levels of language management. Language preferences for menus and dialogs as well as for viewing and typing text can be configured on a system-wide level, or they can be set on an application-by-application basis. Configuring system languages on a global scale is a fairly straightforward task. Aside from choosing a system language at the onset of OS X's installation process, you can configure system language preferences within the Language tab within the International preference pane.

Here's how it's done: If you look closely at the Language tab portion of the International preference pane, you will notice that it is broken into two sections. For the exam, we will be focusing in on the upper portion. By default, this section contains a list of seven languages, and to the right of the list is the following text: Drag languages into your preferred order for use in application menus and dialogs. This roughly translates to whatever language is at the top of the list will become the default language for the entire OS. To add additional languages, click the edit button and a sheet will be displayed with additional language selections. Figure 6.2 depicts the Language tab portion of the International preference pane.

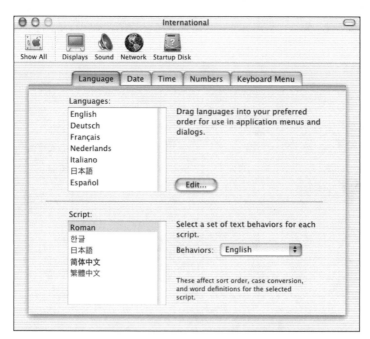

Figure 6.2   The Language tab of the International preference pane.

The somewhat trickier task is to configure the language preferences for a specific application. This is done within the Info window of a selected application from within the Finder. Typically, the Info window contains a pop-up menu that you can use to navigate to the following subcategories: General Information, Name & Extension, Languages, and Privileges. Figure 6.3 illustrates the languages portion of the Info window of the QuickTime Player application. Within the Languages section of the Info window, you will also see a list of available system languages. The list of languages is alphabetized and cannot be reordered. The application's language selection can be altered by checking and unchecking the boxes adjacent to the languages.

Let's say, for example, you want to open QuickTime up in French, but only QuickTime. You would need to highlight the QuickTime player within the Finder, choose Show Info from the File menu (Command+I), and select Languages from the pop-up menu. Next, you would uncheck the all the languages except for French. This task can be executed regardless of whether the application is active or inactive, but, in order for the language change to take effect for an application that is active, you will need to quit and relaunch the application. Upon restart, the application will open in the desired language, which in this instance is French, as shown in Figure 6.4.

In the event that more than one language is checked within the Language section of the Info window, the preferred language of the application will be determined by the order of the languages within the Language tab of the International preference pane. Let's say, for example, that both Spanish and French are checked within the Info window of the QuickTime Player, and the order of languages within the Language tab of the International preference pane is as follows: English, Deutsch, Español, Français, Nederlands, Italiano, and Chinese (refer to Figure 6.2). Upon launching, QuickTime's default language would be Spanish (see Figure 6.5).

Figure 6.3   The Languages portion of the Show Info window of the QuickTime Player application.

Figure 6.4 QuickTime en Français.

Figure 6.5 QuickTime en Español.

Note: Essentially, at any given whim, any aspect of Mac OS X can accommodate customized language preferences, with one exception. AppleCare Knowledge Base Article ID: 106478 states that within Mac OS 10.1, the Login Panel language can only be selected during the initial installation of Mac OS X.

Setting up Login Items

Login items within Mac OS X are roughly the functional equivalent of Mac OS 9's startup items. Login items are managed within a System Preference pane called Login.

The Login preference pane consists of two tabbed subsections: Login Window and Login Items. The Login Window tab can configure Mac OS X to automatically log in to a specific user account upon startup. It also provides various options for the appearance of the Login Window. The Login Items tab enables you to select applications or documents that will be automatically launched upon logging in. These items are account specific, meaning that each user account can have its own customized login items.

Administration of this section is quite simple: Login items are added via the Add button and by selecting the desired login items via a file navigation dialog box, or by dragging and dropping the desired startup item into the Login Items tab section of the Login preferences pane. Login items are removed by highlighting the undesired login items and clicking the Remove button.

Another feature of the Login Items screen is the ability to re-order the launching of login items. This is accomplished by dragging the login items into the desired order of launch. Finally, login items can be hidden after launch by simply placing a check mark in the Hide column next to the intended item. Figure 6.6 depicts the Login Items tab of the Login preference pane.

Figure 6.6   The Login Items tab of the Login preference pane.

Managing Fonts

Mac OS X handles fonts quite differently from Mac OS 9. Unlike OS 9's single Fonts folder, which resides in the System Folder, Mac OS X has multiple font folders that are located throughout the system. Where the fonts are installed will determine which user accounts have access to them. Chapter 4 touched on the concept of search paths and how they apply to fonts. Let's continue forward and examine more closely how this concept works.

The concept of search paths stems from the Mac OS X's security model. A simple way of looking at Mac OS X's security model is to compare it to the security model of network file sharing. Within network file sharing, it is possible to have various user accounts and groups that have different levels of file access on a server. This is analogous to Mac OS X in the sense that it, too, has user accounts and groups with various levels of file access. However, its security model not only applies to network access but to local system access as well. Just as users who cannot access files on a server that they do not have permission for, OS X protects its local content in like manner. This is the security model in which Mac OS X protects a user account's data content from being inadvertently accessed by another user. This is also how OS X protects its system components from being tainted by unruly software and user incompetence.

Simply stated, a *search path* is a hierarchically ordered acquisition of system resources. This hierarchy stems from Mac OS X's security model. In general, most search paths work their way from user-account-specific resources to system-wide resources.

Within Mac OS X, it is possible to have four or more Fonts folders. The number of Fonts folders is predicated on the total number of users and whether or not the Classic application environment has been installed. Refer to Table 6.1 for a more detailed look at how this works. The Fonts folders have been listed in correct search order.

Note: If multiple OS 9 System Folders are present, Mac OS X will only recognize the Fonts folder of the System Folder that is selected for the Classic application environment. Also, note that although Mac OS X applications can access the Fonts folder of the Classic application environment, Classic applications cannot access fonts outside of their own environment.

Mac OS X supports many different font technologies, including Mac and Windows PostScript, Mac and Windows TrueType, and Windows Open Type formats. Although this is not tested on the exam, PostScript Type 1 Multiple Master Fonts are not supported within Mac OS X. Also, as a result of OS X's advanced Quartz graphics-rendering system, Adobe Type Manager is no longer needed for the proper rasterization of PostScript fonts.

The actual process of installing fonts is quite simple. Just copy or drag the desired font files into an accessible Fonts folder assigned to your user account. Currently, in

Table 6.1 A detailed look at the search path for fonts.	
Search Path (Owner)	Location/Additional Information
~/Library/Fonts (User)	The fonts within the Fonts folder inside the Library folder inside the User's home folder is specific to the user account. The resulting user account has complete control over all font items within this location.
/ Library/Fonts (Local)	The fonts within the Fonts folder inside the Library folder inside the root of the volume are shared by all user accounts and are not required by the operating system to run. The font items in this location can only be administered by a system admin account.
/Network/Library/Fonts (Network)	The fonts within the Fonts folder inside the Library folder on the network are shared among all users of a given server. These font resources are usually administered by that server's admin.
/System/Library/fonts (System)	The Fonts folder inside the Library folder inside the System folder contains the default fonts required by the operating system and cannot be altered. (Only the root account has permission to alter the contents of this folder.)
Mac OS 9 Fonts folder (Classic)	Depending on whether Classic is installed and where it resides on the volume, these fonts are not only accessible to the applications that run within the Classic application environment, they are accessible for all of OS X as well. When installing Mac OS X over a preexisting OS 9 installation, fonts are not automatically transferred into OS X's Fonts folders. They will continue to reside within the OS 9 System Folder and will be accessed accordingly.

order to get fonts to be recognized within an open OS X application, you will need to quit and relaunch all open applications in order to make them accessible within those programs.

NetInfo Manager Utility

New to the Mac OS is OS X's utilization of directory services. Directory services provide a consolidated user list that can be shared among multiple network services or servers for authentication. Directory services do not provide the services themselves but rather describe how they are set up. Sharing user data is a more efficient way to administer network resources. It reduces the number of services/servers that need administration in the event that user data changes. Users and groups are maintained in a database, referred to as a *directory*. Typical information that is stored in a directory is user name, password, and user ID. An example of a service that can take advantage of directory services is email. In order for a user to gain access to a mail server, login information must be provided, such as user name and password that matches the information stored within that server's directory.

Directory services within Mac OS X are based on a plug-in architecture. By default, Apple ships plug-ins for NetInfo and Lightweight Directory Access Protocol version 2 (LDAPv2), although it is expected that additional plug-ins for directory services such as Microsoft's Windows Active Directory and Novell's NDS eDirectory will be available for purchase from third-party manufacturers.

NetInfo is the native directory for Mac OS X. A NetInfo database/directory is referred to as a *domain*. The NetInfo database is hierarchical and contains both local and network user as well as group authentication information. All Mac OS X systems contain local user account information, referred to as the *local domain*. Information that resides within the local domain is only visible to the computer it resides on. Because the data stored within NetInfo is hierarchical, when queried for directory services, searches are handled from the local domain outward. This is what is referred to as a *search policy*.

Figure 6.7 shows the Directory Setup application located within the Utilities folder in the Applications folder, which is the program for configuring directory services. The Services pane lists all available directory service plug-ins installed. To configure a directory service, you will first need to click the padlock icon in the lower-left corner of the Directory Services pane and authenticate with an Admin login and password. To enable a service, place a check mark in the Enable column next to the desired service. To configure a service, select the service and click the Configure button. Each plug-in has its own setup interface and will need to be configured, as appropriate.

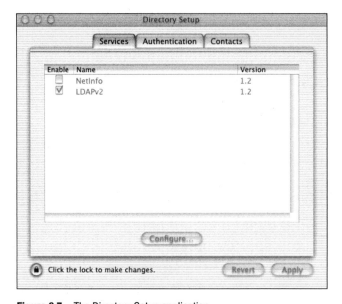

Figure 6.7   The Directory Setup application.

When configured correctly, directory access–capable applications can reference the Directory Setup application for appropriate configurations, although some applications, such as email clients and OS X's Address Book, have their own built-in facilities for accessing directory services and do not utilize the Directory Setup application. Further discussion of network services is beyond the scope of the material of the exam, although there is one last point to cover.

Enabling the Root Account

It is necessary to know how to enable the root account within Mac OS X. The root account is enabled through the NetInfo Manager application. The NetInfo Manager application is a holdover in functionality and appearance from NeXT's OpenStep OS. A word of caution: NetInfo Manager is not an application to dabble in leisurely (joy riding). Like the root account, it is possible to affect changes that have negative consequences. To enable the root account within the NetInfo Manager application, you will need to open the NetInfo Manager application located inside the Utilities folder within the Applications Folder. Next, unlock the padlock icon in the lower-left corner of the NetInfo Manager pane and authenticate with an Admin login and password. Continue forward by selecting Security from the Domain menu and Enable Root from the submenu. After acknowledging the warning message that appears, you will be prompted to supply the root account with a password. After doing so, you will then be prompted to verify the password in order to complete the procedure. Figure 6.8 depicts the NetInfo Manager application. If you forget this procedure, do not panic. You will not be required to recite it verbatim. Half the battle is knowing that the root account is enabled through the NetInfo Manager application.

That wraps up the review of the NetInfo portion of the exam. The second test within the ACTC certification, Mac OS X Server Essentials (Exam 9l0-501), delves more deeply into the workings of NetInfo within a server environment.

Configuring Printers via the Print Center

Mac OS X has a completely different printing architecture as compared to previous Apple desktop operating systems. Within Mac OS 9, printing is *primarily* managed via the Chooser and the Print Monitor. Within Mac OS X, printing is managed via a single application called the Print Center, shown in Figure 6.9, which is located inside of the Utilities folder within the Applications folder. There are no equivalent Desktop Printing and Printer Sharing within OS X. The Print Center supports both networked and local printers. Network printers can be either AppleTalk or LPR (line printer) IP based, whereas local printers are connected via Universal Serial Bus (USB).

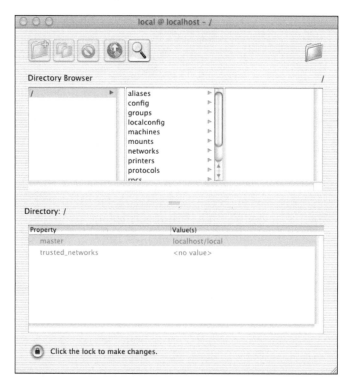

Figure 6.8   The NetInfo Manager application.

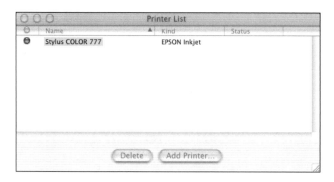

Figure 6.9   Mac OS X's Print Center application.

When the Print Center is first launched, it will search for all supported printing devices. In order for a printer to be recognized, its corresponding print module must be installed. *Print module* is Mac OS X's terminology for printer driver. By default, Mac OS X ships with numerous print modules supporting both Apple and many third-party printers. To install a printer, click the Add Printer button, and you will be presented with a sheet (OS X's equivalent to an OS 9 dialog box) that contains a pop-up menu that lets you choose the type of printer you are adding: AppleTalk, LPR, IP, USB, and Directory Services.

AppleTalk-Based Printers

In order to connect to an AppleTalk-based printer, the AppleTalk networking protocol must first be enabled within the Network preference pane. If this is not the case, you will be presented with a sheet that prompts you to do so. To ease the facilitation of this task, the sheet provides a button that is a shortcut to open the Network preference pane. Once you have enabled AppleTalk, and you have made your printer selection, the Print Center will attempt to determine the printer type and bind the corresponding printer description to your selection. You are also provided the ability of manually selecting the appropriate printer description.

LPR-Based Printers

To connect to an LPR printer, you will need to provide the printer's IP address or DNS name equivalent as well as manually select the appropriate printer model.

USB-Based Printers

Overall, USB printers should provide the least resistance during setup (provided that the appropriate printer module has been installed). Similar to the setup process of AppleTalk-based printers, the Print Center will attempt to determine the printer type and bind the corresponding printer description to your selection. You are also provided the capability of manually selecting the appropriate printer description.

Directory Services

The Directory Services option lists printers and printer queues that are available through NetInfo or LDAP directory services. You will most likely encounter directory services in larger and more intricately structured networking environments.

Once the printer has been configured, you will notice a dot to the left of the name. This dot indicates that this is the default printer. If there are several printers available to choose from, and a different printer is desired as the default instead of the one currently selected, simply choose the desired printer by clicking it and then choose Make Default from the Printers menu.

To determine the status of a print job, you must double-click the printer name within the printer list in the Print Center. The status window will only display the status of print jobs for the current logged-in user. The status window provides the ability to hold, resume, and delete jobs in a queue.

One of the major enhancements within OS X is its utilization of the Portable Document Format (PDF) for Quartz two-dimensional (2D) graphics rendering and printing. In actuality, when you click Preview or Print, a temporary PDF document is generated and utilized for display or output purposes, respectively. Such

PDFs can be saved without the utilization of third-party software, such as Adobe Acrobat, by selecting Save as File Format PDF within the Output Options portion of a typical print dialog in OS X.

 In the event that a document needs to be printed to a printer that's not supported by OS X, Apple recommends saving the document as a PDF, utilizing the preceding specified method, and rebooting into OS 9 and printing from there.

Implementing FireWire and USB Peripherals

Mac OS X ships with broad native support for utilizing FireWire/1394 and USB devices. These peripherals range the gambit from USB mice and keyboards, to digital still cameras and removable media drives, to FireWire hard disks and digital video (DV) cameras. These drivers are typically generic and may lack some of the more advanced features that the installation of manufacturer-supplied software may provide. As a benefit of Macintosh's use of USB and FireWire technology, most Mac OS X external peripherals are plug-and-play devices and therefore do not require a system reboot to be utilized.

Note: Prior to Mac OS X, version 10.0.4, PCMCIA cards (PC cards) were unsupported.

In regard to external local storage, whether removable or fixed, Mac OS X defaults ownership to whoever is logged in at the time.

Practice Questions

Question 1

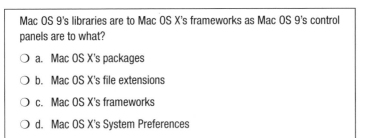

Mac OS 9's libraries are to Mac OS X's frameworks as Mac OS 9's control panels are to what?

- O a. Mac OS X's packages
- O b. Mac OS X's file extensions
- O c. Mac OS X's frameworks
- O d. Mac OS X's System Preferences
- O e. Mac OS X's Directory Services application

The correct answer is d. Mac OS 9's libraries are to Mac OS X's frameworks as Mac OS 9's control panels are to Mac OS X's System Preferences. Mac OS X's System Preferences are the functional equivalent of Mac OS 9's control panels. Answer a is incorrect because a package is a series of files that comprise the underpinnings of a specific application and are represented by a single icon within the Finder. Answer b is incorrect because file extensions are "Internet-friendly" designations included in the name of a file in order to help associate it with its appropriate parent application. Answer c is incorrect because "frameworks" is just another name for packages. Answer e is incorrect because the Directory Services application is used to configure directory services within Mac OS X; it has no functional equivalent within Mac OS 9.

Question 2

True or false: OS X system languages can be configured on a system-wide scale as well as on an application-by-application basis?

- O a. True
- O b. False

The correct answer is a. Mac OS X has language support for both system-wide and application-by-application configuration.

Question 3

What is the minimum number of Font folders in a Mac OS X system that uses Classic?

○ a. One

○ b. Two

○ c. Three

○ d. Four

○ e. None of the above

The correct answer is c. Within Mac OS X, it is possible to have three or more Fonts folders. The number of Fonts folders is dependent on the total number of users and whether the Classic application environment has been installed. Typically, an OS X system will have the following Fonts folders: ~/Library/Fonts (User), /Library/Fonts (Local), /Network/Library/Fonts (Network), /System/Library/fonts (System), and Mac OS 9 Fonts folder (Classic). The /Network/Library/Fonts (Network) Fonts folder is dependent on network resource availability, and the Mac OS 9 Fonts folder (Classic) is dependent on whether the Classic application environment is installed. It is possible to have more than one Mac OS 9 System Folder installed on a Mac OS X system, but OS X can only access the one that has been designated to the Classic application environment.

Question 4

Which font formats have native support in OS X?

○ a. Mac and Windows PostScript, Mac TrueType, and Windows Open Type formats

○ b. Mac and Windows PostScript, Mac and Windows TrueType, and Windows Open Type formats

○ c. Mac PostScript, Mac TrueType, and Windows Open Type formats

○ d. None of the above

The correct answer is b. Mac OS X supports Mac and Windows PostScript, Mac and Windows TrueType, and Windows Open Type formats. Answers a and c are incorrect as a result of omitting a Mac OS X–supported font technology. Answer d is incorrect as a result of answer b being correct.

Question 5

> Which of the following are native directory services of OS X? [Check all correct answers]
>
> ❑ a. LDAP
>
> ❑ b. NDS eDirectory
>
> ❑ c. NetInfo
>
> ❑ d. Windows Active Directory
>
> ❑ e. None of the above

The correct answers are a and c. LDAP and NetInfo are the only natively supported directory services shipped with Mac OS X. Answers b and d are incorrect because NDS eDirectory and Windows Active Directory are not natively supported directory services of Mac OS X, although there may be future support through third-party software development. Answer e is incorrect as a result of answers a and c being correct.

Question 6

> The root account is activated via what application?
>
> ○ a. System Preferences application
>
> ○ b. NetInfo Manager application
>
> ○ c. Directory Services application
>
> ○ d. Users preference pane
>
> ○ e. Universal Access preference pane

The correct answer is b. The root account is activated via the NetInfo Manager application. Answer a is incorrect because the System Preference application has no bearing on the activation of the root user account. Answer c is incorrect because the Directory Services application is used to configure directory services within Mac OS X. Answer d is also incorrect. Although the Users preference pane can administer most user accounts, it does not have the ability to administer the root user account. Answer e is incorrect because the Universal Access preference pane is used to overcome disabilities with the utilization of the mouse and keyboard.

Question 7

True or false: OS X–supported printers are configured via the Chooser?

○ a. True

○ b. False

The correct answer is b. Within Mac OS X, both local and network printers are configured and administered via the Print Center application.

Question 8

What type of printers does Mac OS X support? [Check all correct answers]

❏ a. LPR

❏ b. USB

❏ c. Directory Services

❏ d. AppleTalk

❏ e. All of the above

Answer e is correct. Mac OS X has the following printer support: LPR, IP, USB, Directory Services, AppleTalk.

Question 9

> What types of external peripheral connections does Mac OS X officially support on currently shipping Macintosh computers? [Check all correct answers]
>
> ❑ a. USB
>
> ❑ b. Mac Serial
>
> ❑ c. FireWire
>
> ❑ d. SCSI
>
> ❑ e. Parallel

The correct answers are a and c. Because currently shipping Macintosh computers only ship with USB and FireWire ports, it can be inferred that these are the only external peripheral ports that Mac OS X supports without the utilization of third-party hardware. Answers b and d are incorrect. Although Mac OS X has some limited support for built-in Serial and SCSI, these are external peripheral connections that are not available on currently shipping Macintosh computers without the use of third-party hardware. Answer e is incorrect because Macintosh computers have never shipped with parallel support. Therefore, there is no OS X support for this bus standard.

Need to Know More?

 The Apple Knowledge Base is the definite resource for researching Apple technical support issues. It can be found at **http://kbase.info. apple.com/.**

Check out Article ID 60862, titled "Mac OS X 10.0: Managing AppleTalk Printers."

Check out Article ID 106233, titled "Mac OS X 10.0: Alert Message -9781 When Printing."

Check out Article ID 106290, titled "Mac OS X 10.0: About The Root User And How To Enable It."

Check out Article ID 106417, titled "Mac OS X 10: Font Locations And Their Purposes."

Check out Article ID 106473, titled "Mac OS X 10.1: FireWire Drives Do Not Become Available (Mount) When Connected."

Check out Article ID 106474, titled "Mac OS X 10.1: Select A USB Startup Disk With Startup Manager, Not System Preferences."

Check out Article ID 106478, titled "Mac OS X 10.1: Login Panel Language Only Selectable During Installation."

Check out Article ID 106484, titled "Mac OS X 10.1: Viewing And Typing Text In Different Languages."

Check out Article ID 106490, titled "Mac OS X 10.1: Many Third-Party Ink Jet Printer Drivers Are Included."

Check out Article ID 106512, titled "Mac OS X 10.1: Stops Responding During File Transfer Between FireWire Drives."

Check out Article ID 106516, titled "Mac OS X 10.1: Includes PPDs For Many PostScript Printers."

Check out Article ID 106540, titled "Mac OS X 10.1: Set Up Non-USB Printers After Updating."

Check out Article ID 106557, titled "Mac OS X 10.1: Mac Help Cannot Open System Preferences Pane After An Update Install."

 The OS X Apple Developer site is a good Web resource for additional OS X technical information. Visit it at **http://developer.apple.com/ macosx**.

Check out Technical Note TN2024, titled "The Mac OS X Font Manager."

 The article "Inside Mac OS X: Preference Panes" provides interesting insights into the workings of Mac OS X's preference panes. It can be found at **http://developer.apple.com/techpubs/macosx/Additional Technologies/PreferencePanes/PreferencePanes.html**.

Networking
and File Sharing

Terms you'll need to understand:

✓ Port

✓ Protocol

✓ BootP

✓ AirPort

✓ Topology

✓ PPPoE

✓ Proxies

✓ AFP

✓ Web sharing

✓ Remote login

✓ Share points

✓ Privileges

Techniques you'll need to master:

✓ Administering the Network preference pane

✓ Using the Internet Connect application

✓ Understanding Mac OS X file sharing

✓ Logging in to a server

✓ Knowing the Mail application

The principal theme of Mac OS X's networking is *simplification*. For those who are unfamiliar with Apple's previous desktop OS offerings, its networking component is best described as cobbled together in an ad-hoc fashion. This criticism is not aimed at the underlying technologies of Mac OS 9's networking (which I will leave in the domain of developers to quarrel over) as much as it is directed at its interface and its administration.

In previous iterations of Apple desktop operating systems prior to OS X, networking was managed through a series of control panels. The type of network and protocol dictated which combination of control panels were applicable. Within Mac OS 9, the control panels included AppleTalk, Dial Assist, File Sharing, Internet, Location Manager, Modem, Remote Access, TCP/IP, and Web Sharing. The administration of Apple's AirPort wireless technology did not adhere to this paradigm. It instead utilized three independent applications (AirPort Setup Assistant, AirPort, and AirPort Admin Utility) in conjunction with a control strip module. Also, let's not forget the mechanism of connectivity to Apple Filing Protocol (AFP) servers. This was handled with yet another set of applications located in the Apple Menu—referred to as the *Network Browser*; it's really an alias to an item located within the Applications (Mac OS 9) folder—and the Chooser. Neither of these applications is dependent on the other to function, although one thing they have in common is that they both employ additional subordinate software pieces to provide their functionality.

Within Mac OS X, Apple streamlines the entire process into three separate system preference panes called Internet, Network, and Sharing. AFP connectivity is handled directly within the operating system's Finder.

This chapter focuses on the following topics: administration of networking, connectivity to AFP file servers, configuration of peer-to-peer file sharing, and how to set up an email account.

Administering the Network Preference Pane

The Network preference pane is responsible for configuring all networking preferences within Mac OS X. In order to modify the Network preference pane, you will need to be logged in as an admin user or you must unlock the padlock button in the lower-left corner of the Network preference pane. This is done by clicking the padlock button and supplying a valid admin user's name and password. Due to Mac OS X's industrial-strength modern underpinnings, changes take effect immediately and do not require a system restart.

Similar to the layout of other system preference panes, the Network preference pane consists of several subsections that are divided by tabs. The available subsections/tabs are dependent on the type of network port that has been selected for configuration.

Ports

Simply stated, a *port* (as referred to within the Network preference pane) is some form of physical connection to a data network. Typically, the network ports you will encounter are Internal Modem, Built-in Ethernet, and AirPort. To select a network port, it is necessary to click the pop-up menu adjacent to Show:, as depicted in Figure 7.1. In addition to the aforementioned varieties of network ports is a selection called Active Network Ports (interfaces). The Active Network Ports selection brings up a configuration screen that allows for the activation, deactivation, creation, duplication, and deletion of available network ports. It also allows for the ordering of port preference when a Mac OS X system attempts to connect to a network.

To activate or deactivate a port, click the box next to the desired port. A box that has a check in it means that its port is active. To change the order of the ports that Mac OS X will utilize when attempting to connect to a network, simply click and

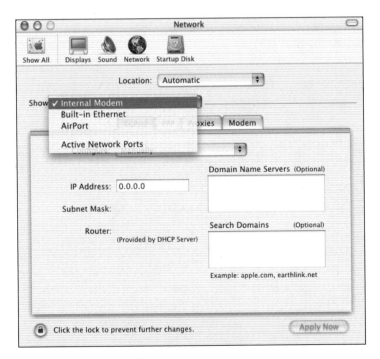

Figure 7.1 The port selection pop-up menu.

hold the desired port and drag it into your preferred order. To change a port name, simply double-click the appropriate port and enter the desired name. To delete a port, select the intended port and click the Delete button. Figure 7.2 shows the Active Network Ports configuration screen within the Network preference pane.

In addition to deleting ports, it is possible to add a new port or duplicate an existing port. Typically, you would add or duplicate a port as a result one of the following conditions:

➤ A port needs to be created after you physically add a new network connection, such as a network interface card (NIC) or a modem.

➤ The Mac OS X system is portable, and its ports need to be configured to accommodate networking for different locations.

When a new port is created or duplicated, it will be added to the pop-up menu adjacent to Show label. Conversely, when a port is deactivated or deleted, it will be removed from the pop-up menu adjacent to Show:. After you make the desired modifications to Active Network Ports and close the Network preference pane, you will be prompted with a Save dialog box requesting your confirmation of the configuration changes.

Figure 7.2 The Active Network Ports configuration screen.

Protocols

Another term you need to know is *protocol*. Simply stated, in networking a protocol (sometimes referred to as a *communication protocol*) is a set of rules for the exchange of data between computer systems. As stated previously, the port being administered will determine what subsections/tabs are available for configuration. The majority of these tabbed subsections deal with protocol configurations, with the exception of tabbed subsections that refer to hardware configuration or proxies. Let's examine all the tabs, starting with the protocols first.

The TCP/IP Tab

As shown in Figure 7.3, the TCP/IP tabbed subsection of the Network preference pane is basically the functional equivalent to Mac OS 9's TCP/IP control panel. Because Mac OS X is supposedly the most Internet-savvy microcomputer operating system of all time, by default it has been configured to utilize TCP/IP as its preferred networking protocol. TCP/IP can be configured over all varieties of network ports. This includes built-in Ethernet, third-party Ethernet NICs, the internal modem, third-party USB modems (both digital and analog), as well as AirPort and its third-party supported equivalents.

Figure 7.3   The TCP/IP tab.

When you're administering TCP/IP via Ethernet or AirPort, regardless of whether it's Apple supplied or from a third party, an address can be configured by means of four different options: Manually, Manually Using a DHCP Router, Using DHCP, and Using BootP. Although you probably won't ever use this option, BootP (the Bootstrap Protocol) maps out a particular TCP/IP address to a particular computer. This is accomplished by utilizing the Ethernet port's unique Media Access Control (MAC) as a point of reference for anchoring the designated TCP/IP address. The BootP option might be advantageous in NetBoot environments, where a machine does not consistently boot from its internal hard disk and a particular TCP/IP address is desired for a particular workstation.

The configuration of TCP/IP via a modem is also a straightforward process. Regardless of whether the modem is Apple supplied or from a third party, digital or analog, TCP/IP can only be configured by two options: Manually or Using PPP. If you have experience configuring TCP/IP within Apple's previous desktop operating systems, Mac OS X should pose no problem. However, if you require a more detailed explanation on how to configure TCP/IP within Mac OS X, check out another Coriolis book, Mark R. Bell's *The Mac OS X Book: The Ultimate Macintosh User's Guide,* for additional how-to information.

The AppleTalk Tab

By default, OS X ships with AppleTalk turned off. For the most part, I have seen users enable it only to facilitate printing to an AppleTalk network printer. However, another reason might be to connect to a legacy AFP server that does not have support for the TCP/IP protocol (although this is only supported in Mac OS X 10.1 and above). One final reason, remote as it may be, is to provide support for legacy Mac OS clients when hosting peer-to-peer file sharing.

On a couple of occasions, I have come across people who confuse AppleTalk with LocalTalk. The former is a protocol, and the latter is a networking topology. A *topology* is a description of a physical arrangement or layout of networking hardware. LocalTalk network connectivity is unsupported under Mac OS X. As with the TCP/IP tabbed portion of the Network preference pane, the AppleTalk portion should provide little or no challenge to you if you are familiar with Apple's previous desktop OS offerings. Figure 7.4 shows the AppleTalk tab within the Network preference pane.

 Although protocols can be configured to use separate network ports, it is totally possible to configure multiple protocols for the same port. For example it is possible to configure both the protocols of AppleTalk and TCP/IP to share a single Ethernet port.

Figure 7.4   The AppleTalk tab.

The PPP Tab

Point-to-Point Protocol (PPP) is an industry standard for the communication of computing devices over dial-up plain-old telephone (POTS) lines and Basic Rate Interface (BRI) Integrated Services Digital Network (ISDN) lines. The PPP tab is only available when you're configuring analog and ISDN modem ports. As mentioned with the other protocols, familiarity with Mac OS 9's PPP control panel will provide you with great insight into the administration of the PPP tabbed subsection of the Network preference pane, although it's not essential.

One thing worth mentioning, besides the initial PPP setup options you will encounter when administering the PPP tabbed subsection, are the additional/advanced options that can be configured via the PPP Options button at the bottom of the preference pane. Simply click the button and a sheet will be displayed with the additional options. Within the PPP Options sheet, you can enable the option Connect Automatically When Starting TCP/IP Applications. Figure 7.5 shows the PPP tab within the Network preference pane.

The PPPoE Tab

Just as the name states, Point-to-Point Protocol over Ethernet (PPPoE) is simply an implementation of PPP over Ethernet. Although not always the case, PPPoE is used primarily with Digital Subscriber Line (DSL) and cable modem services.

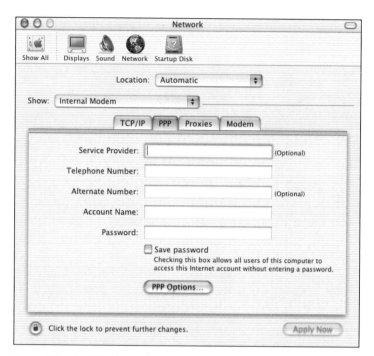

Figure 7.5 The PPP tab.

Typically, an ISP will require PPPoE when it wants to regulate access or meter usage of its subscribers. As the name implies, PPPoE works only with Ethernet ports. When PPPoE is enabled, it disables AppleTalk on the port being utilized.

Previous to OS X, Apple did not supply PPPoE connectivity software with its OS offerings. Historically, ISPs who required PPPoE provided it by means of third-party software. In Figure 7.6 you will notice that the configuration information requirements for the PPPoE tab are quite similar to that of the PPP tab, with the exception of supplying a telephone number to dial.

A useful and interesting addition to Mac OS X 10.1 is the ability to show PPPoE status in the menu bar. This feature is activated by simply placing a check in the box adjacent to Show PPPoE Status in Menu Bar at the bottom of the PPPoE tabbed subsection of the Network preference pane. When enabled, this feature places an icon representing an Ethernet connection within the menu bar at the top of the screen. When clicked, this icon will display a drop-down menu containing the following information:

➤ The PPPoE status

➤ The ability to initiate or terminate a connection

➤ A shortcut for opening the Internet Connect application.

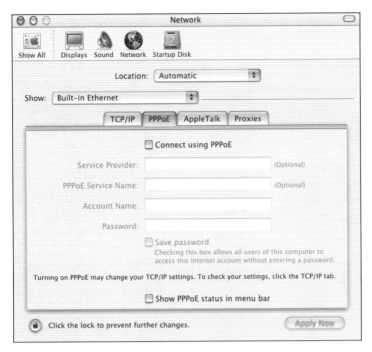

Figure 7.6   The PPPoE tab.

The Proxies, Modem, and AirPort Tabs

Although they do not represent protocols, Proxies, Modem, and AirPort are all tabbed subsections that can be administered within the Network Preference pane.

The configuration of proxies deals with network security, and Proxies is an available tabbed subsection for most network ports. A proxy typically employs a server that acts as an intermediary between a user's workstation and the Internet. When a request is made for Internet content, the request is passed along to the proxy server. The proxy server will then act on behalf of the client and forward or block, (depending on the rules set on the proxy server) the request to the Internet and if allowed will relate the retrieved response back to the user. Proxy servers are primarily used for various security reasons or in conjunction with a cache server appliance for improved Internet performance. As a matter of course, when configured correctly, the use of proxies will be transparent to the user.

When administering the Proxies tab, as shown in Figure 7.7, you will need to know the appropriate address and port information for the intended proxy server. In this reference, a *port* is an assigned connection place associated with a network service. Here, ports are represented by numeric values. For example, port 80 represents an HTTP (Web) service. The Proxies tab allows you to enable proxies on a service-by-service basis as well as bypass them for specific server address or for the retrieval of data via FTP.

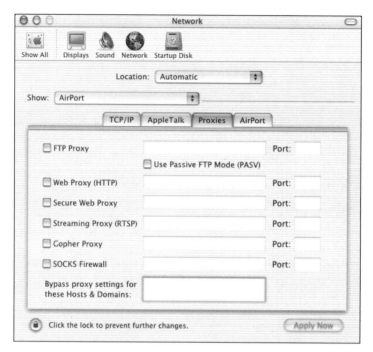

Figure 7.7 The Proxies tab.

The Modem tab, shown in Figure 7.8, is the functional equivalent of Mac OS 9's Modem control panel and, as it stands, is administered in like fashion.

If you want to initiate a modem connection manually, you can do so with the Internet Connect application located inside the Applications folder. The Internet Connect application obtains its settings from the PPP tabbed subsection of the Network preference pane. Additionally, it provides the ability to add additional phone numbers to dial as well as an entry field for manually entering your login password for your ISP, if you did not supply it within your PPP configuration information. Figure 7.9 depicts the Internet Connect application while administering modem configurations.

Not to be confused with AirPort (the physical networking port), the AirPort tab, shown in Figure 7.10, is a subsection of the Network preference pane. It can only be accessed when configuring the AirPort physical port. It allows you to select the preferred network, the network password, and Show AirPort Status in Menu Bar. This last item places an icon representing the AirPort signal strength within the menu bar. When clicked, this icon will display a drop-down menu with the following selections:

➤ AirPort: On with Turn AirPort Off

➤ AirPort: Off with Turn AirPort On

➤ Current Selected Network

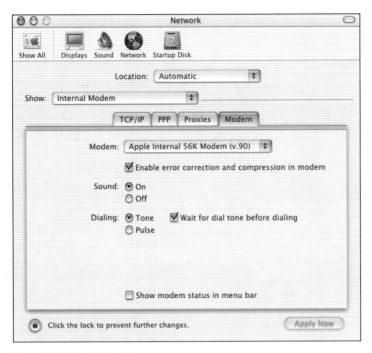

Figure 7.8 The Modem tab.

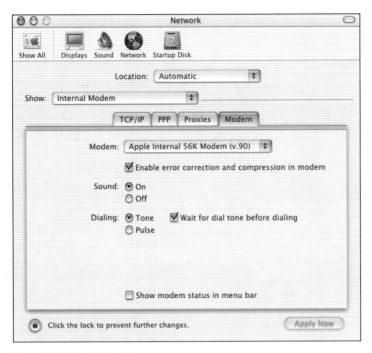

Figure 7.9 The Internet Connect application.

➤ Other (which allows for the entry of the name and password for a closed AirPort network)

➤ Create Network (which allows for the creation of a computer-to-computer network)

➤ Open Internet Connect

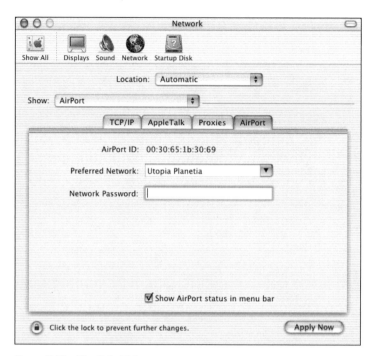

Figure 7.10 The AirPort tab.

Locations

Locations are Mac OS X's equivalent to Mac OS 9's Location Manager. Locations allows for the creation of a single point of reference for the administration of a defined set of network ports and the configuration of the networking protocols (such as TCP/IP and AppleTalk) that run on those ports. This single point of reference allows for the simplification of management of multiple ports and their assigned protocols when you're utilizing a Mac OS X system in multiple locations. For example, you might be a PowerBook-wielding road warrior and work out of multiple locations, such as New York and Boston offices as well as your home office located somewhere in the suburbs of New Jersey—and let's not forget that hotel in Cambridge, Massachusetts. Locations allows for a convenient way of organizing the multiple network configurations that would be required for successful connectivity at all these locations.

By default, Mac OS X's installer setup creates a location called Automatic. The Automatic location sets all available network ports to active status and then allows OS X to automatically utilize the appropriate port to make a successful network connection. To select, create, or edit (using Duplicate, Rename, or Delete) a location, click the pop-up menu adjacent to Location:, as shown in Figure 7.11. Although any user account within Mac OS X can select any location, new or additional locations can be created only by an admin user account.

This can be accomplished either by logging in to the system as an admin user, or by unlocking the padlock at the lower-left corner of the Network preference pane, and authenticating as an admin user from within a normal logged-in user account. If you are creating a new location, name it appropriately (for example, Home, Office, Mobile, and so on) and then click the OK button to confirm. Once this is completed, the new location will be listed within the pop-up menu adjacent to the Locations label.

Besides being able to choose a location from within the Network preference pane, you can also select a location from within the Apple menu, under the submenu Location, as shown in Figure 7.12. Within the Location submenu, you will also find a shortcut for the Network preference pane, aptly named Network Preferences.

The final thing you will need to know about the operation of the location feature is that the administration of ports and protocols within the Network preference pane is only applicable to the location from where they are being edited. This means that for every location, you can have a completely independent set of configurations for any existing port and its binding protocols. Let's say, for example, you have two locations: Home and Office. At your residence, you have the good fortune of utilizing a cable modem for your Internet connection, which you connect to via Ethernet. While at your office, both network and Internet connectivity

Figure 7.11 The Locations pop-up menu located within the Network preference pane.

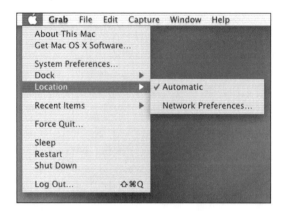

Figure 7.12   The Location submenu located under Mac OS X's Apple menu.

are also aggregated via Ethernet. To alleviate the necessity of having to reconfigure your built-in Ethernet settings every time you change locations, you would create two separate locations—one for your home and one for your office. To keep things consistent we'll name these locations Home and Office. Within each location you would configure the Ethernet port and its binding protocols appropriately. In other words, when the Home location is selected, the Ethernet port will have its own settings independent of how it has been configured from within the Office location. Therefore, two totally separate Ethernet port configurations exist—one for home and one for the office.

*Note: Multiple ports configured for the same location behave as follows: Let's say, for example, more than one active modem port is configured for the same location within a single OS X system. When Mac OS X fails to make a successful connection utilizing the first modem port, **it will not** attempt to reconnect utilizing the second modem port. Instead, it will make an attempt utilizing the next non-modem port within the active ports list.*

AFP File Server Connectivity

Although Mac OS X supports a variety of server technologies (AFP, SMB/CIFS, WebDAV, and NFS), to keep this book's text focused on exam material, we will be covering the AFP variety. Prior to Mac OS X 10.1, AppleTalk was not a supported protocol for AFP connectivity. In order to use the AppleTalk protocol, make sure it is enabled within the Network preference pane. Mac OS X relies on a network service discovery system referred to as *Network Services Location* (NSL).

Server connectivity is handled directly in the Finder. To connect to a server, simply select Connect to Server (Command+K) from the Go menu, and you will be presented with a network service navigation window similar in functionality to that of Mac OS 9's Network Browser.

At the top of the Connect To Server window is a pop-up menu that will allow for the selection of recent server connections. At the center of the Connect To Server window is a mechanism for visually navigating to available network servers. Typically, you will only see a selection called Local Network. Local Network allows for the selection of networked volumes made available by the NetInfo directory service. If NetInfo is not being utilized, the only volume that will appear with Local Network is the *localhost* (a generic term for the computer being operated from). Local Network can also be accessed from within a Finder window (by clicking Computer from the Finder window's toolbar). Furthermore, if AppleTalk is enabled, you will also be presented with the option of navigating to AFP volumes that are available through the AppleTalk protocol. Finally, at the bottom of the Connect To Server window is an entry field for the manual input of a server address if needed. Figure 7.13 shows the Connect To Server window.

To disconnect a server, select the intended volume by clicking it and choosing the **Eject** command (Command+E) from the File menu. You can also disconnect by clicking and dragging the intended volume over the trash icon in the Dock. As this is done, you will notice that the trash icon becomes an eject icon. Mac OS X does away with the longstanding **Put Away** command (Command+Y) found in previous iterations of Macintosh operating systems.

Administering the Sharing Preference Pane

Mac OS X offers a number of ways to share information across a network. These methods include FTP serving, peer-to-peer file sharing via AFP, Secure Shell (SSH) remote login, and Web sharing (HTTP). The administration of file sharing is done

Figure 7.13   The Connect To Server window.

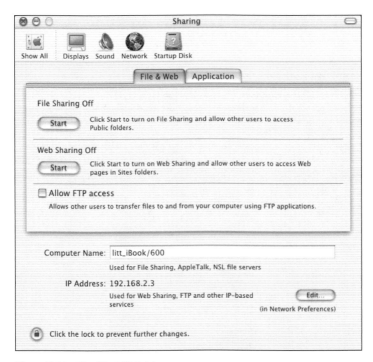

Figure 7.14   The File & Web tab.

through the Sharing preference pane. The Sharing preference pane has two tabbed subsections: the File & Web tab and the Application tab. As you can see in Figure 7.14, the File & Web tab provides the facility to start and stop file sharing and Web sharing, and it also allows FTP access.

As shown in Figure 7.15, the Application tab allows for the enabling of remote login via a terminal application that supports SSH. It also provides a control mechanism for the enabling of Allow Remote Apple Events, which allows AppleScript programs running on other computers to interact with your computer. The bottom portion of the Sharing preference pane allows for the specification of what the computer's name will be for use with File Sharing, AppleTalk, and NSL file servers. It also displays the system's current IP address and an Edit button, which is a shortcut to the Network preference pane.

File Sharing

Peer-to-peer file sharing can take place via AFP utilizing either AppleTalk or TCP/IP protocols for connections. When activated, file sharing is enabled system-wide for all users on the host machine. Due to the necessity to create a marketable distinction between Mac OS X and Mac OS X Server, Apple limits the total number of simultaneous connections to 10. Anything greater will require the purchase of Mac OS X Server (if one were to stick within the Apple product line).

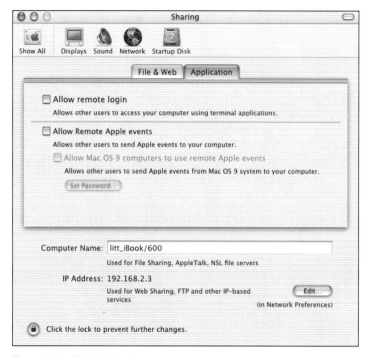

Figure 7.15   The Application tab.

*File sharing should not be confused with local file sharing between local user accounts, which is done via the **Shared folder** located in the Users folder.* By default, Mac OS X provides a single point of access for each user's share contents. This is referred to as a *share point* and cannot be altered through the GUI (another distinction between Mac OS X and Mac OS X Server). Content that is to be shared over a network should be placed within a user's Public folder.

By default, Mac OS X enables read-only guest access for each user's Public folder (see Figure 7.16).

There is also a Drop Box folder within each user's Public folder. The Drop Box is configured with write-only privileges for all, with the exception of the user account to whom it belongs (see Figure 7.17).

The configuration of privileges for the Public folder allows the contents to be viewed remotely without the liability of having them accidentally modified, overwritten, or deleted. To make modifications to a shared item, it would need to be copied off onto the client machine. The configuration of privileges for the Drop Box folder provides a safe haven for remotely connected users to place content on the machine in a secure manner without the prying eyes of other remotely connected users.

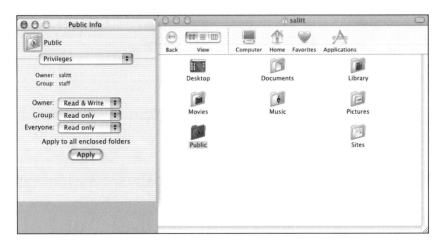

Figure 7.16 Privilege configurations for the Public folder.

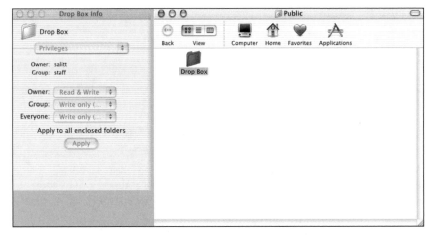

Figure 7.17 Privilege configurations for the Drop Box folder.

Note: To limit access to local user accounts only, click the user's Public folder and select Show Info (Command+I) from the File menu. Then click the pop-up menu at the top of the window and select Privileges. Next, set the access for Everyone to None.

Typically when a guest logs in to a Mac OS X file sharing host, he will be presented with a list of publicly available share points for all the user accounts on that computer. When a local user account logs in, not only will he be able to access the contents of the publicly available share points, he will be able to access his own machine contents, as if he were logged in the computer locally.

Web Sharing

Web sharing allows you to make use of Mac OS X's built-in Apache Web server. As shipped, Apple places administration restrictions on the advanced features of the Apache Web server within Mac OS X. This is yet another distinction between Mac OS X and Mac OS X Server. Ultimately, it is Apple's desire for you to upgrade to Mac OS X Server if you require more feature-rich file serving. Like file sharing, when activated, Web sharing is enabled for all users simultaneously. Each user account can host its own site, and content that is to be shared should be placed in ~/ Sites (the user's home directory Sites folder). Access to the content would be obtained through a Web browser by entering **http://host_machines_IP_address/ ~username** as the URL. A system-wide site can also be configured by placing the content to be shared within /Library/WebServer/Documents, which can be accessed by simply utilizing the hosts IP address as the URL.

Remote Login

Before enabling remote login, consider upgrading to the latest version of Mac OS X. Initially when OS X shipped, there was no provision for SSH (encrypted logins and passwords) via terminal applications. Once remote login is enabled, only local user accounts have the ability remotely log in. If a remote login is needed by someone who does have a user account on the local host, you will have to create one through the Users preference pane.

FTP

FTP serving is an excellent way of serving files agnostically to different computing platforms. Mac OS X's implementation of FTP has no anonymous/guest access, and like remote login, FTP access requires a user account on the local host machine. If FTP access is needed by someone who does have a user account on the local host, you will have to create one through the Users preference pane.

Mail

Mac OS X has a built-in mail application. Aptly named Mail, it is a full-featured mail client for Post Office Protocol (POP), Internet Message Access Protocol (IMAP), and Unix mail servers. The Mail application can also serve as a client for Apple's iTools service, also referred to as a *Mac.com account*. During Mac OS X's installation process, if you create new or supply existing iTools user account information, the Setup assistant will automatically configure the Mail application appropriately. If you have not done so, a Mac.com account can easily be obtained at a later date by clicking the Signup button at the bottom of the iTools tabbed subsection of the Internet preference pane, which is the same as visiting http://itools.mac.com using a Web browser. Finally, if you supply existing iTools user account information within the iTools tabbed portion of the Internet preference pane, the account will automatically be configured within the Mail application. Figure 7.18 depicts the Mail application (Mac OS X's built-in email client).

Figure 7.18   The Mail application.

Practice Questions

Question 1

> Which of the following ports can be utilized with a location?
>
> ○ a. AirPort
>
> ○ b. Ethernet
>
> ○ c. Modem
>
> ○ d. All of the above

The correct answer is d. A location can utilize all port types. These include but are not limited to AirPort, Ethernet, and Modem connections.

Question 2

> True or false: PPPoE can be configured within the AirPort connection in the Network preference pane.
>
> ○ a. True
>
> ○ b. False

The correct answer is b. This is a false statement. The name says is all: Point-to-Point Protocol over Ethernet (PPPoE) can only be configured for an Ethernet connection.

Question 3

> Which of the following are types of email accounts that the Mail application can support? [Check all correct answers]
>
> ❏ a. IMAP
>
> ❏ b. iTools
>
> ❏ c. Mac.com
>
> ❏ d. POP
>
> ❏ e. Unix

The correct answers are a, b, c, d, and e. The Mail application has built-in support for IMAP, iTools/Mac.com, POP, and Unix mail accounts. If you were confused between answers b and c, don't be. They are the same thing.

Question 4

> Which of the following are examples of ports?
>
> ❏ a. Modem
>
> ❏ b. Ethernet
>
> ❏ c. AirPort
>
> ❏ d. All of the above

The correct answer is d. Modem, Ethernet, and AirPort are all physical network connections, which by definition are ports.

Question 5

> The terms *AppleTalk* and *TCP/IP* refer to what?
>
> ○ a. Ports
>
> ○ b. Protocols
>
> ○ c. Proxies
>
> ○ d. Share points

The correct answer is b. AppleTalk and TCP/IP are networking protocols. Answer a is incorrect because a port is either a physical connection to a network or an assigned connection place associated with a network service represented by numeric value. Answer c is incorrect because in Mac OS X, the term *proxies* refers to servers that act as intermediaries between a user's workstation and the Internet. Answer d is incorrect because in Mac OS X, *share points* are designated points of remote data across a network in conjunction with Mac OS X's various file-sharing services.

Question 6

> The location that shares data among local users is called _____.
>
> ○ a. Drop Box
>
> ○ b. Public
>
> ○ c. Shared
>
> ○ d. None of the above

The correct answer is c. The Shared folder is the location for sharing data among local users. Answer a is incorrect because the Drop Box folder provides a secure location for remotely connected users to share data with a local user account. Answer b is incorrect because the Public folder is the location where a local user would share data openly with remote connected users. Answer d is incorrect as a result of answer c being correct.

Question 7

How many built-in ways can Mac OS X share data across a network?

○ a. Four

○ b. Six

○ c. Eight

○ d. Ten

○ e. None of the above

The correct answer is a. Mac OS X has four separate ways it can share data across a network. Mac OS X can share data via FTP serving, peer-to-peer file sharing via AFP, Secure Shell (SSH) remote login, and Web sharing (HTTP). Some might argue that email is also a way of sharing data, but it can be countered with the argument that although Mac OS X provides a mail client, it is a separate application from the OS. Answers b, c, d, and e are incorrect as a result of answer a being correct.

Question 8

What is the maximum number of simultaneous file-sharing connections Mac OS X is capable of?

○ a. Two

○ b. Four

○ c. Six

○ d. Eight

○ f. None of the above

The correct answer is f. Mac OS X can support up to 10 simultaneous file sharing connections. Answers a, b, c, and d are incorrect as a result of answer f being correct.

Need to Know More?

 The Apple Knowledge Base is the definite resource for researching Apple Technical support issues. It can be found at **http://kbase.info.apple.com/**.

Check out Article ID 60058, "Mac OS X Server: What Is BootP?"

Check out Article ID 106224, "Mac OS X 10.0: File Sharing Only Shares Only Shares Public Folders."

Check out Article ID 106260, "Mac OS X 10.0: Computer Name Does Not Appear on Network."

Check out Article ID 106262, "Mac OS X 10.0: Connecting to AppleShare or File Sharing Requires TCP/IP."

Check out Article ID 106282, "Mac OS X 10.0: Setup Assistant Does Not Accommodate DSL User Name and Password."

Check out Article ID 106298, "Mac OS X: Using AppleTalk with PPPoE."

Check out Article ID 106432, "Mac OS X: DSL/PPPoE Frequently Asked Questions (FAQ)."

Check out Article ID 106433, "Mac OS X 10.0: Frequently Asked Questions (FAQ) for PPP Modem Connections."

Check out Article ID 106439, "TCP and UDP Ports Used by Mac OS X Services."

Check out Article ID 106461, "Mac OS X: File Sharing."

Check out Article ID 106472, "Mac OS X: FTP, SSH, and Telnet Require BSD Subsystem."

Check out Article ID 106483, "Mac OS X and Mac OS X Server: Compatible Network Media."

Check out Article ID 106546, "Mac OS X 10.1: Re-enter Mail Password After Upgrade."

Check out Article ID 106568, "Mac OS X 10.1: Protocols That Can Be Used With 'Connect to Server.'"

Check out Article ID 106593, "Mac OS X: AirPort May Be Called 'Ethernet (Slot 1)' or 'en1.'"

Check out Article ID 106599, "Mac OS X: Selecting Sharing Pane Causes System Preferences to Quit Unexpectedly."

Check out Article ID 106631, "Mac OS X: Some Services Cause Modem Connection During Startup."

Check out Article ID 106608, "Mac OS X 10.1: AppleTalk Does Not Work After Being Enabled."

Check out Article ID 106613, "Mac OS X: 'No AppleTalk printers are available' Message."

Check out Article ID 106646, "Mac OS X: 'Error Code -37' When Copying Files to Earlier AppleShare Servers."

Classic

Terms you'll need to understand:

✓ Chooser
✓ Control panels
✓ Classic preference pane

Techniques you'll need to master:

✓ Starting Classic
✓ Shutting down Classic
✓ Printing from Classic
✓ Administering Classic

As discussed in Chapter 2, one of the major stumbling blocks Apple faced in its quest to build a modern operating system was how to maintain compatibility for legacy software programs. In fact, regardless of the platform, at one time or another every major OS has faced the challenge of its own evolution while maintaining compatibility with its existing software base. The Classic application environment, sometimes referred to as the *TrueBlueEnvironment*, is Apple's technology that provides the essential hinge pin that allows Mac OS 9 users to successfully migrate to Mac OS X. The Classic application environment allows legacy Macintosh software applications to operate simultaneously with Mac OS X native applications, thus easing the transition for existing longtime Macintosh users. The reference to legacy software programs means pre–Carbon application programming interfaces (APIs). Simply stated, an API provides the way in which an application makes a request of the OS or another application. A Carbon application contains the minimum API requirement to take advantage of Mac OS X's modern OS features and to not rely on the Classic application environment for its functionality.

The Classic application environment provides Mac OS X the ability to run Mac OS 9 and its applications in a self-contained process that is relatively transparent to the user. If an application can run in Mac OS 8 or 9, it is a safe bet that it will run within the Mac OS X Classic application environment. For the most part, the only limitation the Classic application environment places on Mac OS 8 and 9 applications is direct access to hardware device control. To overcome this limitation, Apple recommends booting the system back into Mac OS 9 when necessary.

Note: One word of caution: Mac OS 9 does not respect Mac OS X's security features, and booting from Mac OS 9 will expose a Mac OS X system to security risks, such as prying eyes or even data loss. This actually exposes a major security hole within Mac OS X. Even if you went as far as to eliminate Mac OS 9 from all your local volumes, there is still the potential of booting from a Mac OS 9 Installer CD—or for that matter myriad external Mac OS 9 boot options—which will defeat Mac OS X's security features.

Apple states that you will need a minimum of Mac OS 9.1 and Startup Disk control panel 9.2.1 to utilize the Classic application environment. Apple also states that Mac OS 8 and 9 applications can be installed directly from the Classic application environment, thus eliminating the need to boot into Mac OS 9. However, you should pay special attention to make sure the installer's destination folder is accessible in accordance with Mac OS X's security model.

When Classic is first started (and depending on your iteration of Mac OS 9), a number of OS components are copied into the Mac OS 9 System Folder. These systems components include updates to the Startup Disk control panel, the

AppleScript Extension, and a number of new files, such as Classic, Classic Rave, Classic Support, and Classic Support UI. The files are the conduits that allow Mac OS 9 to make system calls within Mac OS X.

Note: One way you can identify when you are operating in the Classic application environment is the fact that applications will take on Mac OS 9's Platinum appearance.

As for printing through the Classic application environment, you will need to have the appropriate OS 9 printer drivers installed as well as be familiar with the utilization of the Mac OS 9 Chooser. As a rule of thumb, you will find that if a printer manufacturer states that its products are Mac compatible, it is talking about OS 9 rather than OS X. To make your OS X transition easier, try to select a printer that has drivers for both Mac OS 9 and Mac OS X.

Finally, as stated in Chapter 3, special attention is needed when dealing with Classic and UFS-formatted volumes. Unix File System (UFS) volumes do not show up when booted from Mac OS 9, their volume names cannot be customized, and a special procedure is required before the Classic application environment can run from them. One more important limitation to know about the UFS format is that Mac OS 9 files may not read correctly when OS X's command line is used.

The Classic Preference Pane

The Classic preference pane is the central point in which the Classic application environment is administered. It is divided into two tabbed subsections: the Start/Stop tab and the Advanced tab.

Start/Stop

The Start/Stop tab allows for the selection of the Mac OS 9 system that will be utilized by the Classic application environment. It also provides the option Start Up Classic On Login To This Computer, in addition to the ability to start, restart, and force-quit the Classic application environment on demand. Figure 8.1 shows the Start/Stop tab of the Classic preference pane.

Note: Classic can also be started from the GUI simply by opening a non–Carbonized Mac OS 8 or 9 application. Another noteworthy piece of information is that Carbonized applications provide the option of selecting the preferred environment in which to open. This provides the user the choice of having Carbonized applications open in Mac OS X or the Classic application environment. To make this selection, you will need to get information (Command+I) on the Carbonized application, and, depending on your preference, you will need to check or uncheck the box adjacent to Open in the Classic Environment. This is done from the General Information pop-up menu.

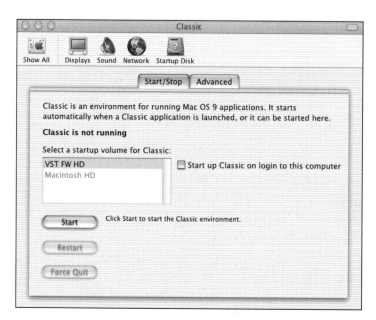

Figure 8.1 The Start/Stop tab of the Classic preference pane.

Advanced

The Advanced tab provides some useful options for optimizing the Classic application environment's performance. The Advanced tab is divided into three sections: Startup Options, Put Classic To Sleep When It Is Inactive For, and Other Classic Utilities.

Through a pop-up menu, the Startup Options section can be used to configure Mac OS 9 to turn off extensions during Classic's startup (the equivalent of holding down the Shift key during OS 9's startup), open the Extensions Manager during Classic's startup (the equivalent of holding down the spacebar during OS 9 startup), and use Key Combination. Key Combination allows the Classic app to emulate the depression of Mac OS 9 during the Classic environment's startup. This is useful for extensions or control panels that respond to pressed key combinations during Mac OS 9's startup process (such as Casady & Greene, Inc.'s Conflict Catcher). You can configure up to five keys within a combination, and there is a Clear Keys button in the event you want to modify or eliminate the key combination altogether. Finally, the Start Classic button allows you to immediately activate Classic, implementing whatever selection you have made within the Startup Options pop-up menu. Figure 8.2 shows the three available selections within the Startup Options portion of the Advanced tab.

Because the Classic application environment is one of the more processor-intensive applications within Mac OS X, the Put Classic To Sleep When It Is

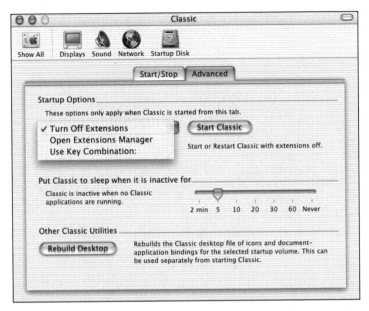

Figure 8.2   The Advanced tab of the Classic preference pane. (Take note of the available selection of Startup Options within the tab.)

Inactive For option is especially useful because it allows the Classic app to be put into a state of hibernation in order to reduce the load on system resources. Within this section, you can specify the duration of time before the Classic app is put to sleep when it is inactive. The time frequency ranges from 2 to 60 minutes, in addition to an option to never put Classic to sleep. This ability allows for more efficient utilization of memory and the CPU when the Classic app is inactive. When the Classic app is recalled for duty, it automatically comes back online with no need for any user intervention.

The last section in the Advanced tab is Other Classic Utilities. In this section, you will be provided the facility to rebuild Mac OS 9's desktop file. Within Mac OS 9, a volume's desktop file contains the metadata (the descriptive information) of icons and document application bindings for that particular volume. Be prepared to become a professional progress bar watcher, because this option, although useful, takes quite some time to execute even with a limited amount of Mac OS 9 data on the specified volume.

Mac OS 9 Control Panels

The control panel is Mac OS 9's functional equivalent of Mac OS X's System Preferences Application. Mac OS 9's control panels can be delineated into two varieties: Apple supplied and third party supplied. For review purposes, we will only focus on the Apple-supplied variety. OS 9's control panels are located in a

Table 8.1 Mac OS 9 control panel functionality when utilized from the Classic application environment.		
Fully Functional	**Partially Functional**	**Nonfunctional**
Apple menu option	Appearance	Control Strip
AppleTalk	File Synchronization	DialAssist
ColorSync	General Controls	Energy Saver
Date & Time	Keyboard	File Sharing
Extensions Manager	Memory	Infrared
File Exchange	Monitors	Location Manager
Internet	Sound	Modem
Keychain Access	USB Printer Sharing	Mouse
Launcher		Multiple Users
Numbers		Password Security
QuickTime Settings		PowerBook SCSI Disk Mode
Software Update		Remote Access
Speech		Startup Disk
Text		TCP/IP
		TrackPad
		Web Sharing

Note: Software Update is only functional when utilizing Mac OS 9.2.1 as Classic's OS in conjunction with MAC OS X 10.1.

folder aptly named Control Panels. This folder is located inside the Mac OS 9 System Folder. When utilized from the Classic application environment, not all of Mac OS 9's control panels are functional. Table 8.1 contains a breakdown of the functionality of the Mac OS 9 control panels when utilized from the Classic app. Administrative changes made in Mac OS 9 control panels do have a global affect within Mac OS X. These changes solely apply to the behavior of Mac OS 9 within the Classic application environment and will carry forward when Mac OS 9 is the system startup OS.

 The Classic application environment is designed in such a way that it relies upon Mac OS X's System Preferences application for some of its configurations, as in the cases with TCP/IP and Display preferences. Conversely, *not a single* Mac OS 9 control panel has influence outside the Classic application environment.

Practice Questions

Question 1

> Which is not a limitation of running Classic off a UFS-formatted volume?
>
> ○ a. Desktop printing is nonfunctional.
>
> ○ b. Volume names cannot be customized.
>
> ○ c. Mac OS 9 files may not read correctly from the command line.
>
> ○ d. None of the above.

The correct answer is a. Desktop printing is unaffected by the UFS format. It is nonfunctional regardless of the variety of volume format. Answer b is incorrect because the inability to customize UFS is definitely a limitation of UFS-formatted volumes. Answer c is incorrect because the potential inability to read Mac OS 9 files is definitely a limitation of UFS-formatted volumes. Answer d is incorrect as a result of answer a being correct.

Question 2

> Which of the following can be configured from the Classic preference pane?
>
> ○ a. Login Items
>
> ○ b. AppleTalk
>
> ○ c. TCP/IP
>
> ○ d. None of the above

The correct answer is d. None of these items can be configured from the Classic preference pane. Answer a is incorrect because Login Items is configured from the Login preference pane. Also, Mac OS 9 Startup Items is an alias placed in the Startup Items folder within the Mac OS 9 System Folder. Answer b is incorrect because AppleTalk is administered via the Network preference pane as well as via Mac OS 9's AppleTalk control panel. Answer c is incorrect because TCP/IP is administered through the Network preference pane.

Question 3

> True or false: While running Classic, TCP/IP can be configured from within Mac OS 9.
>
> ○ a. True
> ○ b. False

The correct answer is b. Classic disables Mac OS 9's TCP/IP control panel. All TCP/IP configurations are handled through the Network preference pane.

Question 4

> True or false: When booted in Mac OS 9, any system software changes that are made through the control panels will have an effect within the Classic application environment.
>
> ○ a. True
> ○ b. False

The correct answer is a. Control panels that function within the Classic app will retain configuration changes between Mac OS 9 and the Classic application environment.

Question 5

> With regard to printing, which of the following Mac OS 9 printer components are still applicable when used with the Classic application environment? [Check all correct answers]
>
> ❏ a. Chooser
> ❏ b. Desktop printing
> ❏ c. PrintMonitor
> ❏ d. Printer Descriptions
> ❏ e. None of the above
> ❏ f. All of the above

The correct answers are a, c, and d. Mac OS 9's Chooser, PrintMonitor, and Printer Descriptions all retain functionality with the Classic application environment. Answer b is incorrect because desktop printing does not function within the Classic app. Answers e and f are incorrect as a result of answers a, c, and d being correct.

Question 6

> What is the minimum OS 9 revision required for use with the Classic application environment in OS X 10.0 on a Blue & White G3?
>
> ○ a. 9.0
>
> ○ b. 9.0.4
>
> ○ c. 9.1
>
> ○ d. 9.2.1
>
> ○ e. 9.2.2

The correct answer is c. OS 9.1 is the minimum revision of Mac OS 9 that can be used with the Classic application environment on a Blue & White G3. Answer a and b are incorrect because OS 9.0 and 9.0.4 are not certified to function with the Classic application environment. Answers d and e are also incorrect. Although OS 9.21 and 9.2.2 will function with the Classic application environment on a Blue & White G3, neither one is the minimum requirement for functionality.

Question 7

> Which of the following are legitimate ways to start up Classic? [Choose all correct answers]
>
> ❑ a. By opening a non-Carbonized application.
>
> ❑ b. By opening a non-Carbonized application using Login Items during login.
>
> ❑ c. By enabling the Start Up Classic on Login to This Computer feature from the Classic preference pane
>
> ❑ d. All of the above

Trick question!

The correct answer is d. All these specified methods can be used to start up the Classic application environment. Opening a non–Carbonized application using Login Items during login will produce the same results as opening a non–Carbonized application on demand.

Need to Know More?

 The Apple Knowledge Base is the definite resource for researching Apple technical support issues. It can be found at **http://kbase.info.apple.com/**.

Check out Article ID 25305, "Mac OS X 10.0.x: Using Mac OS 9 Control Panels in Classic Environment."

Check out Article ID 106155, "Mac OS X 10.0: Cannot Connect to AOL in Classic Environment."

Check out Article ID 106170, "Mac OS X 10.0: Classic Does Not Allow Direct Hardware Networking Access."

Check out Article ID 106179, "Mac OS X 10.0: Mac OS 9.0.4 Classic Requires Update to Mac OS 9.1 or Later."

Check out Article ID 106182, "Mac OS X 10.0: Cannot Capture Video in Classic."

Check out Article ID 106183, "Mac OS X 10.0: Some Classic Applications Require Installation of System Folder Components."

Check out Article ID 106184, "Mac OS X 10.0: Access Not Provided in Classic for Certain Hardware-Oriented Applications."

Check out Article ID 106185, "Mac OS X: Copy and Paste Between Classic and Mac OS X Applications."

Check out Article ID 106225, "Mac OS X 10.0, Mac OS 9.1: Update Startup Disk Control Panel to 9.2 or Later."

Check out Article ID 106249, "Mac OS X 10.0: Unexpected Classic Behavior when Using Mac OS 9.1 All or Base Extension Sets."

Check out Article ID 106276, "Mac OS X 10.0: Classic Does Not Allow Use of Software Update."

Check out Article ID 106277, "Mac OS X 10.0: Classic Does Not Work from a UFS Disk First Use."

Check out Article ID 106278, "Mac OS X 10.0: You Are Running Classic without Superuser (root) Privileges."

Check out Article ID 106281, "Mac OS X 10.0: Theater Mode Extension May Prevent Use of Other Applications."

Check out Article ID 106399, "Mac OS X 10.0: Pointer Disappears while Using Classic Application."

Check out Article ID 106518, "Mac OS X: Classic Startup Graphics Incorrect with Video Mirroring."

Check out Article ID 106572, "Mac OS X 10.1: Grey Screen when Attempting to Start Classic Environment."

Check out Article ID 106580, "Mac OS X 10.1: How to Use iDisk in Classic."

Check out Article ID 106601, "Mac OS X 10.1: The 'Classic Environment Is Not Responding' Message."

Troubleshooting and Support

· ·

Terms you'll need to understand:

✓ Kernel panic
✓ Verbose mode
✓ Process
✓ Split-half
✓ **top**
✓ **fsck -y**

✓ **sudo**
✓ **man**
✓ **pwd**
✓ **ls**
✓ **chmod**
✓ **chown**

Techniques you'll need to master:

✓ Switching between OS X and OS 9
✓ Reselecting a file's parent application
✓ Force-quitting applications
✓ Killing processes
✓ Gathering information
✓ Using the OS X CD as a trouble-shooting tool

✓ Implementing OS X's utilities
✓ Knowing command-line basics
✓ Installing software updates
✓ Reinstalling OS X
✓ Reinstalling OS 9
✓ Understanding basic Apple troubleshooting methodology

When I first began writing this book, Mac OS X was at version 10.0.4. Since then, the product has steadily matured through a series of software updates to its latest revision, 10.1.2. During this period, many bugs and deficiencies were squashed, and a bevy of new features were added to the operating system. Based on my initial experience from taking the exam, in addition to taking into account the latest developments within OS X, I have attempted to anticipate any changes in material that might be tested. Although I have done my best, I cannot make any guarantees because both the OS and the exam itself are moving targets.

This chapter is the final chapter dedicated to the review of exam subject material. It will focus mainly on topics dealing with the troubleshooting and support of Mac OS X. However, I would not describe the material covered within this chapter as an in-depth, end-all guide to troubleshooting and repair of Mac OS X. Instead, I would describe the material as more of a general orientation to the various tools and methodologies that can be applied to the support of Mac OS X.

Switching between OS X and OS 9

Switching between Mac OS X and Mac OS 9 may be one of the most important tools in the quest to support Mac OS X. Although I make every effort to use Mac OS X as my primary OS, I have encountered a few situations that have necessitated a reboot into Mac OS 9. These reasons range from lack of driver support for various pieces of hardware, to running hard disk repair utilities, to the fact that some non-Carbonized applications simply work better when launched directly from an OS 9–booted Macintosh in lieu of utilizing the Classic application environment.

Both Mac OS X and Mac OS 9 have a built-in mechanism to select the desired startup OS. Within both operating systems, this mechanism is referred to as *Startup Disk*. Although the name is Startup Disk, both mechanisms allow for the selection from multiple OS installations within the same partition. In Mac OS X it is the Startup Disk preference pane, as shown in Figure 9.1, whereas in Mac OS 9 it is the Startup Disk control panel, as shown in Figure 9.2.

Note: As stated in Chapter 8, Mac OS 9 requires a minimum of Startup Disk control panel 9.2.1. Also again worth mentioning, OS 9 does not support OS X's security model.

Be aware that as with Mac OS 9's Startup Disk control panel, configurations made within the Startup Disk preference pane have a global effect within Mac OS X. To prevent the selection of a different startup OS from within OS X, lock the padlock at the bottom-left corner of the Startup Disk preference pane. Although this will prevent normal users from making modifications within the Startup preference pane, it will not avert having the machine booted from external media when utilizing startup key sequences such as Boot from External Drive (Command+Shift+Delete), Boot from CD (C), or Startup Manager (Option).

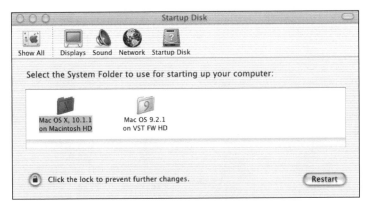

Figure 9.1   Mac OS X's Startup Disk preference pane.

Figure 9.2   Mac OS 9's Startup Disk control panel version 9.2.1.

Note: Chapter 6 touched on the Login preference pane and its two tabbed subsections: Login Window and Login Items. Within the Login Window tab is the option Disable Restart and Shut Down Buttons Within The Login Window. Do not be lulled into the misconception that this is any feasible security measure that would prevent a boot-up from a Mac OS X CD. One would only need to know the proper startup key combinations (that is, Command+Shift+Delete, C, or Option) to circumvent this feature.

Startup Manager, as shown in Figure 9.3, is a feature of New World Architecture Macintosh computer systems. Startup Manager, which is sometimes referred to as *OS Picker*, is enabled by simply holding down the Option key during system

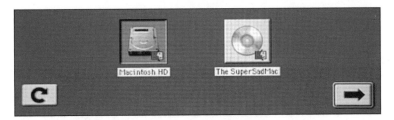

Figure 9.3   The Startup Manager feature of New World Architecture Macs.

startup. Using the Startup Manager, as well as the other aforementioned key sequences, is not a valid way of selecting from multiple OS installations on the same partition.

As of this writing, Apple had just publicly released the software utility Open Firmware Password. This application can enable security features within Open Firmware–compatible Macs that will aid in the prevention of an unauthorized startup from sources other than the designated startup volume. When the Open Firmware Password application's security features are enabled, all startup key sequences, with the exception of the Startup Manager, are disabled. The only distinguishable difference when using the Startup Manager in conjunction with the Open Firmware Password application's security features is that you will be required to provide a password before an alternate startup disk can be selected. For a more detailed explanation, review AppleCare Knowledge Base Article ID 106482, "Mac OS X 10.1: How to Set Up Firmware Password Protection."

Reselecting a File's Parent Application

In Chapter 5, we briefly touched on how to set privileges with Mac OS X's Info window. In actuality, the Info window can serve many functions. The type of item being inspected will dictate the available options you'll have to choose from. As a general rule of thumb, documents (files containing content) will have more available options than folders and volumes.

As stated in Chapter 5, the Info window is accessed by selecting the item within the Finder and choosing the Show Info command under the File menu or by utilizing the key combination Command+I. The Info window's available options are accessed via a pop-up menu. For instance, the following options (subselections) can be accessed from the Info window while inspecting a Word document: General Information, Name & Extension, Open With Application, Preview, and Privileges. Of particular utility is the Open With Application option.

In Chapter 4, in the section titled "File Forks and Extensions," we discussed how files are associated with their parent applications. In the event that a file's preferred parent application is unavailable, or it's simply not opening with the desired application when double-clicked, the Open With Application option provides the ability to reselect the desired parent application.

To reselect a file's parent application, select the intended item within the Finder and choose the Show Info command under the File menu or use the key combination Command+I. Next, select the Open With Application option from the Show Info window's pop-up menu. Here, you will find a pop-up menu that allows for the selection of a different parent application as well as the option to globally apply the selection to files of like type. If you select Change All, you will be presented with a dialog box requesting confirmation. Figure 9.4 depicts the

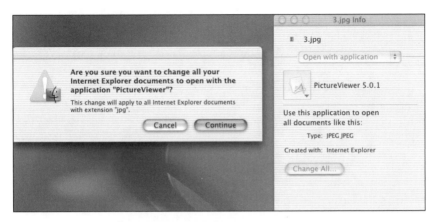

Figure 9.4   The Open With Application option of the Finder's Show Info command and its Change All confirmation dialog box.

Open With Application option of the Show Info command as well as the confirmation dialog box.

Force-Quitting Applications

Force-quitting an application is a way to terminate an unresponsive application without having to restart the computer. Although it was possible to force-quit an application under Mac OS 9, it often led to system-wide instability until the next system restart. Unlike in Mac OS 9, it is possible to force-quit an application without having any negative impact on concurrently running applications within Mac OS X. This is a direct benefit of Mac OS X's modern OS architecture's protected memory feature. In fact, Apple encourages the use of force-quitting applications as a valid tool when applicable to the troubleshooting process; in doing so, Mac OS X provides a systematic way of handling this.

To force-quit an application, you can use either the holdover key combination from Mac OS 9 (Command+Option+Esc), or you can select Force Quit from the Apple menu. You will next be presented with the Force Quit Applications window, shown in Figure 9.5, where all visibly running applications will be displayed.

By "visibly running applications," I mean those that are typically opened by the end user. Unbeknownst to most end users, Mac OS X has a lot of other software activity taking place in the background. This activity involves what are known as *processes*, and these are usually transparent to the end user. Processes can also be force-quit, referred to as "killing a process," which we will cover in the next section. You will surely encounter many applicable situations where force-quitting will be necessary. In fact, you can even force-quit the Finder. This action is referred to as "relaunching the Finder." The next time you are selecting the Finder from within the Force Quit Applications window, take note that the text within the Force Quit button will change to Relaunch.

Figure 9.5 Mac OS X's Force Quit Applications window.

Note: You cannot individually force-quit Classic applications, although you can force-quit the entire Classic Application environment.

Killing Processes

As a simplistic definition, a process can be either an entire program or threads (tasks) within a program. As stated earlier, a process can be force-quit, which in this context is referred to as *killed* or *terminated*. Processes can be killed from either the ProcessViewer application or the command line. For exam purposes, we will be focusing on the ProcessViewer application (see Figure 9.6).

The ProcessViewer application is located within the Utilities folder, inside of the Applications folder. The ProcessViewer provides greater detail and control over the Force Quit command in addition to listing all running processes regardless of whether they are visible. It displays the processes' names, users (the owners of the processes), status, percent memory utilization, and percent processor utilization.

When launched, the ProcessViewer application will list all running processes in the window Process Listing. This window provides a host of sorting options for its contents as well as an option to provide an even greater display of detailed information. Each process is assigned to a specific user; this is what is referred to as *process ownership*. The User column contains the information as to which user owns what process.

In order to kill a process, you will need to own the process. To kill a process, simply double-click it, and you will be presented with a dialog box requesting verification to force-quit the process. This is the equivalent of the **kill** command when using the command line. If by some chance a process cannot be killed, you can terminate it more aggressively by using the Quit Process (Shift+Command+Q) command found under the Processes menu. This is the equivalent of the **kill –9** (definite termination) command when using the command line.

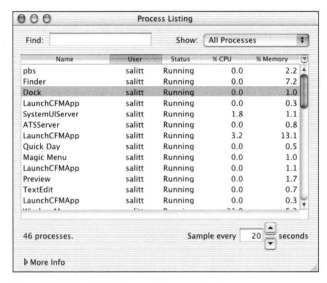

Figure 9.6   Mac OS X's ProcessViewer application.

Information Gathering

Information gathering may be the single most important capability a technical professional can have in his or her repertoire. Regardless of platform, information gathering should be the first step in any troubleshooting methodology. Being a capable information gatherer will enhance your problem-solving abilities in a multitude of ways, including accuracy, timeliness, and completeness. In this section, we are going to review some of key tools Mac OS X provides for information gathering.

Apple System Profiler

Like its OS 9 counterpart, the Mac OS X Apple System Profiler, shown in Figure 9.7, is a very useful utility that provides a summarized report of installed hardware and software of a given Mac OS X system. The Apple System Profiler is located inside of the Utilities folder within the Applications folder. The Apple System Profiler uses a tabbed interface with the following subsections: Applications, Devices and Volumes, Extensions, Frameworks, and System Profile. The major differences between the OS X and the OS 9 versions are the Extensions and Frameworks tabs.

Although the OS 9 version has an Extensions tab, it pertains to system inits, whereas the OS X version's Extensions tab deals with kernel extensions. Kernel extensions provide functionality to the core OS, typically providing access to hardware components such as PCI cards, USB devices, and so on. The information within the Extensions tab is categorized under Name, Version, and Is Apple. As

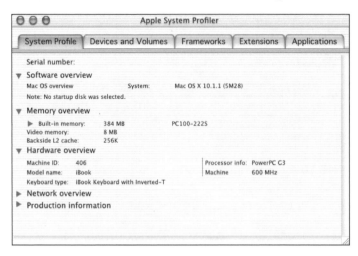

Figure 9.7   The Mac OS X version of the Apple System Profiler.

you might have surmised, "Is Apple" is a category that makes the distinction as to whether an extension is Apple or third party in origin.

A new and unique addition to the Mac OS X version of the Apple System Profiler is the Frameworks tab. As discussed in Chapter 4, Mac OS X frameworks are analogous to Mac OS 9 shared libraries in that they both contain dynamically loading code that is shared among multiple applications. Similar to the functionality of the Extensions tab, the Frameworks tab lists all installed frameworks, along with version numbers and whether or not they are Apple or third-party in origin.

CPU Monitor

If the Central Processing Unit (CPU) is the heart of the computer, then the CPU Monitor is the echocardiogram. The CPU Monitor is an application that graphically displays processor utilization. The CPU Monitor is located in the Utilities folder within the Applications folder. The CPU Monitor application can provide three different graphical representations of CPU usage: Floating, Expanded, and Standard, as shown in Figure 9.8.

The Floating and Standard views are quite similar in that they both display CPU activity in a vertical thermometer-styled usage gauge. The only significant difference between the two views is the amount of screen real estate they utilize. Also, the Floating view has some limited transparency capability. The Expanded view displays a window with a histogram-like graphical representation of processor usage. All three views can be selected from the Processes menu. The Processes menu also has additional options for clearing the Expanded view window, opening the ProcessViewer application, and opening the Terminal application, while

Figure 9.8 The three views of the CPU Monitor (from left to right: Floating, Expanded, and Standard).

```
● ○ ○                    /usr/bin/login (ttyp1)
Processes:  49 total, 3 running, 46 sleeping... 119 threads         00:02:08
Load Avg:  1.08, 0.97, 0.79    CPU usage: 41.7% user, 13.4% sys, 44.9% idl
SharedLibs: num =  110, resident = 26.3M code, 968K data, 7.05M LinkEdit
MemRegions: num = 3550, resident =  111M + 9.21M private, 71.6M shared
PhysMem: 38.9M wired,  186M active,  115M inactive,  340M used, 44.1M free
VM: 1.34G + 51.3M   11866(0) pageins, 1953(0) pageouts

  PID COMMAND     %CPU   TIME   #TH #PRTS #MREGS RPRVT  RSHRD  RSIZE  VSIZE
12541 top          7.8% 0:24.15  1   14     14   212K   352K   320K  1.37M
12535 tcsh         0.0% 0:00.10  1   24     15   436K   680K   900K  5.72M
12515 top          3.9% 0:31.95  1   15     15   224K+  352K   336K+ 1.38M+
12510 tcsh         0.0% 0:00.13  1   24     15   448K   680K   908K  5.72M
11554 Terminal     1.5% 0:53.82  6   93    186   2.01M  9.90M  7.05M 58.6M
 6515 Preview      0.0% 0:07.70  3  112    106   4.89M  6.26M  6.76M 56.7M
 5930 Microsoft    0.0% 0:46.98  2   77    124   5.07M  9.94M  6.45M+ 56.3M
 5928 Microsoft   32.2% 1:51:00  7  128    500   39.3M  47.3M  51.9M  137M
 5277 Quick Day    0.0% 0:00.54  1   61     65   668K   5.82M  1.90M 48.0M
 5268 Quick Cont   0.0% 0:00.58  1   60     60   584K   3.92M  1.79M 45.8M
 5263 MagicMenu    0.7% 0:18.11  1   51     59   584K   5.70M  1.29M+ 47.4M
 5262 CPU Monito   0.0% 7:11.93  3  116    103   1.98M  9.12M  6.82M 58.5M
 5261 iTunesHelp   0.0% 0:00.24  1   46     39   352K   2.72M   952K 30.2M
 5260 Magic Menu   0.0% 0:11.44  1   67     85   2.05M  5.90M  3.68M 54.0M
 5259 SystemUISe   0.7% 6:59.86  3  125    163   2.21M  6.37M  4.43M 55.2M
```

Figure 9.9 The **top** command as entered from within the terminal.

simultaneously issuing the **top** command (see Figure 9.9). The **top** command provides a significantly more detailed view of processor usage within the command line.

Console

The Console application, shown in Figure 9.10, is an information-gathering tool that displays the Mac OS X system.log as entries are being written to it. The Console application is located in the Utilities folder within the Applications folder. The Console application can also be used to display the contents of other logs, such as FTP and NetInfo. The use of logs can be a vital asset in the troubleshooting process.

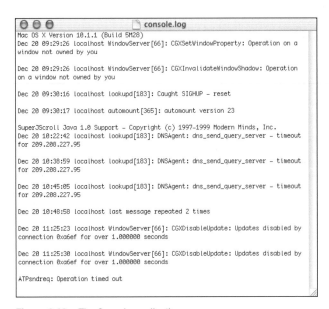

```
○ ○ ○                        console.log
Mac OS X Version 10.1.1 (Build 5M28)
Dec 20 09:29:26 localhost WindowServer[66]: CGXSetWindowProperty: Operation on a
window not owned by you

Dec 20 09:29:26 localhost WindowServer[66]: CGXInvalidateWindowShadow: Operation
on a window not owned by you

Dec 20 09:30:16 localhost lookupd[183]: Caught SIGHUP - reset

Dec 20 09:30:17 localhost automount[365]: automount version 23

SuperJScroll Java 1.0 Support - Copyright (c) 1997-1999 Modern Minds, Inc.
Dec 20 10:22:42 localhost lookupd[183]: DNSAgent: dns_send_query_server - timeout
for 209.208.227.95

Dec 20 10:38:59 localhost lookupd[183]: DNSAgent: dns_send_query_server - timeout
for 209.208.227.95

Dec 20 10:45:05 localhost lookupd[183]: DNSAgent: dns_send_query_server - timeout
for 209.208.227.95

Dec 20 10:48:58 localhost last message repeated 2 times

Dec 20 11:25:23 localhost WindowServer[66]: CGXDisableUpdate: Updates disabled by
connection 0xa6ef for over 1.000000 seconds

Dec 20 11:25:30 localhost WindowServer[66]: CGXDisableUpdate: Updates disabled by
connection 0xa6ef for over 1.000000 seconds

ATPsndreq: Operation timed out
```

Figure 9.10   The Console application.

Verbose Mode

Verbose mode is a built-in feature of Mac OS X that can be used as a system diagnostic during boot up. During Mac OS X system boot up, a lot of activity takes place without being conveyed to the end user. Verbose mode displays all system activity during startup in text format. This activity can include hardware diagnostics as well as the loading of various software and device drivers. Verbose mode can be activated by holding down Command+V at the initial Macintosh startup chime. If all is well, the system will boot into the Aqua GUI. If there is an issue to be dealt with, verbose mode will stop the boot-up process at the point of issue.

Grab

Grab is an alternative to the Mac operating system's traditional built-in screenshot capability. The Grab application is located in the Utilities folder within the Applications folder. When OS X was initially released, the Grab application was the only game in town for taking screenshots within the OS. Even though the screen-grab key sequences (Shift+Command+3 and Shift+Command+4) have returned, the Grab utility still affords additional functionality with a timed capture feature. The timed capture feature, shown in Figure 9.11, is especially useful in capturing choreographed screen activity; it provides a 10-second countdown before a screen capture is taken.

Figure 9.11   The Grab application's Timed Screen Grab dialog box.

Kernel Panic

As a friend of mine once said, "If it can fly, I can crash it." Although Mac OS X's industrial-strength OS workings make it a tough operating system to totally crash, there are some circumstances in which this event can occur. The most prominent system-wide crash is referred to as a *kernel panic*. In Chapter 2, I mentioned that the microkernel is the foundation that provides basic services for all other parts of the operating system. When the microkernel encounters a situation it cannot handle, a kernel panic occurs. Typically, the Macintosh will become nonresponsive, and a series of white text on a black background will be drawn on top of whatever is being viewed on the monitor at the time of the occurrence. Unlike an application crash, within Mac OS X a kernel panic causes a system-wide nonrecoverable lockup. When a kernel panic occurs, the Macintosh system will minimally require a hard system restart (depending on the model, the reset button or Option+Command+power key) to regain functionality. Although it's not required study material, AppleCare Knowledge Base Document 106464, "Mac OS X: Troubleshooting a Startup Issue," provides a treasure trove of useful information that should provide some assistance with kernel panic troubleshooting.

A kernel panic can occur as a result of both hardware and software technical problems. According to Apple Knowledge Base Document 106227, "Mac OS X 10.0: What Is a Kernel Panic?," the information displayed as a result of a kernel panic may furnish developers with useful data for troubleshooting the issue. It also goes on to state that as a result of the kernel panic, you will be unable to record the information by means of taking a screenshot via the OS (the Grab application or Shift+Command+3). Instead, it is recommended that you take a photograph of the screen without the use of a flash. If a camera is unavailable, it is recommended that you copy down the information by hand. Figure 9.12 is a photograph of a kernel panic.

The Mac OS X Install CD

Besides functioning as OS X's installer, the Mac OS X Install CD provides additional functionality as a support tool. For starters, the Mac OS X Install CD has a detailed installer logging feature that can be a useful tool in the diagnosis of

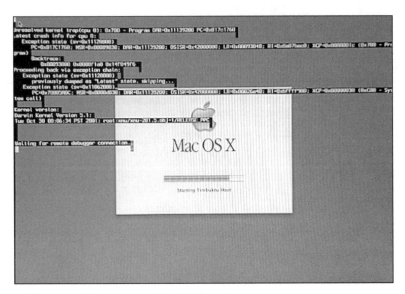

Figure 9.12 A photograph of a Mac OS X kernel panic.

Mac OS X system software installation issues. This feature can only be activated when booted from the Mac OS X Installer CD and by selecting Show Log from the File menu. A log window, shown in Figure 9.13, will be appear at the bottom of the screen that displays details of the installation process as well as any errors encountered. In addition to the installer logging feature, the Mac OS X Install CD can reset forgotten user passwords, verify, repair, erase, and partition a hard disk, and create stripped and mirrored disk arrays.

Disk Utility

Disk Utility is the functional equivalent of combining Disk First Aid and Drive Setup into one application while simultaneously giving it a dose of steroids. I've listed the Disk Utility program under the heading "The Mac OS X Install CD" because it can be accessed via two methods. First, it can be accessed directly from the Macintosh HD from within the Utilities folder inside of the Applications folder. Second, Disk Utility can be launched by booting from the Mac OS X Installer CD and selecting Open Disk Utility from the Installer menu.

The Disk Utility application interface is divided into the following tabbed sub-sections: Information, First Aid, Erase, Partition, and RAID. The Information tab provides statistics and data on how the disk is configured. The First Aid tab, shown in Figure 9.14, can verify and repair the directory structure of a hard disk. It is the graphical equivalent of using **fsck** (file system check) on the command line. For more information about **fsck**, see the section "Command-Line Essentials," later in this chapter. One limitation of the First Aid portion of the Disk Utility app is that it cannot be run on the boot volume. In order to repair the boot

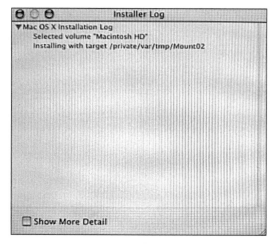

Figure 9.13 Mac OS X's Installer Log window.

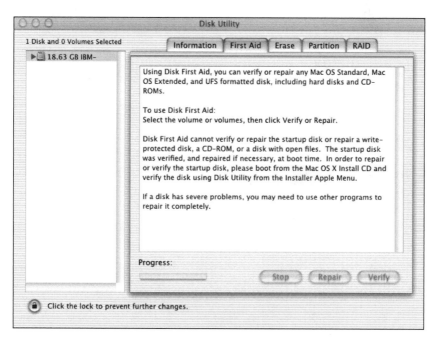

Figure 9.14 The First Aid tab of Mac OS X's Disk Utility.

volume (Macintosh HD), you will need to boot from the Mac OS X Install CD and run the Disk Utility off the Installer CD.

The Erase, Partition, and RAID tabs are the equivalent of Mac OS 9's Drive Setup application with the addition of some of the functionality of the Connor RAID utility that was bundled with old AppleShare IP builds. As with the Disk Utility tab, the Erase, Partition, and RAID tabs cannot be applied to the boot partition. You will need to boot and use the Disk Utility application off of the Mac OS X Install CD in order to use them on the Macintosh HD.

Reset Password

In Chapter 5, you learned that if an admin user forgets her password, it can be reset from another accessible admin user account. However, in the event that the admin user forgets her password and there is no other accessible admin user account, the Mac OS X Install CD can be used to achieve the same result. To do so, you must first boot from the Mac OS X Install CD and select the Reset Password command from the File menu. This will quit the Mac OS X installer and launch a utility aptly titled Reset Password (see Figure 9.15). Next, you will need to select the volume and user account that requires the password reset. You will be required to enter a new password and then reenter it for verification. A word of caution: This method can defeat any existing user account password, including the root account.

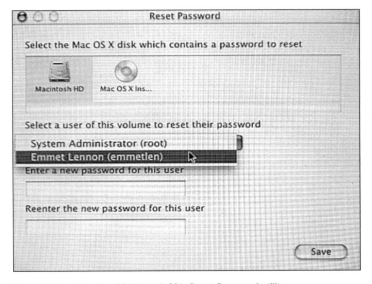

Figure 9.15   The Mac OS X Install CD's Reset Password utility.

Network Utility

The Network Utility provides a useful set of network troubleshooting and diagnostic tools. The application has a multitabbed interface that contains the following subsections: Finger, Info, Lookup, Netstat, Ping, Port Scan, Traceroute, and Whois. For the exam, you will only need to be familiar with the function of the Info, Lookup, Ping, and Traceroute tabs.

Info

The Info tab, shown in Figure 9.16, is probably the Network Utility's most rudimentary tool. It basically provides a general summary of information and statistics about a given network port. In order to obtain information about a specific network interface, you will need to click the pop-up menu and choose the desired interface.

Ping

When I hear the term *ping*, it always conjures up images of submarines and World War II naval movies. The Ping tab, shown in Figure 9.17, works theoretically in a similar fashion to marine sonar. I think of sonar because it uses acoustical pings as a method for providing the echolocation of objects submerged under water. In networking, Ping can be used to validate the connectivity of another IP-aware networking device on the Internet. In order to accomplish this, Ping can send a series of data packets to a designated IP address and listen for a reply—not unlike the theory behind sonar. Ping can also be used as a barometer of performance to determine the speed of a connection. This information can be garnered from the response time between the ping and the reply.

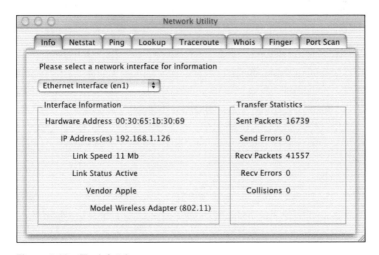

Figure 9.16   The Info tab.

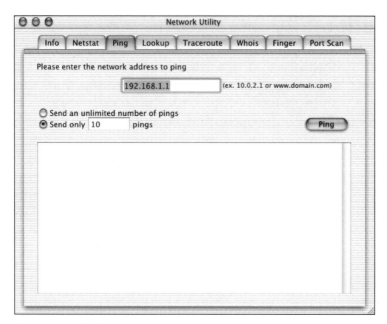

Figure 9.17   The Ping tab.

To use the Ping tool, simply enter an IP address or a domain within the address field in the Ping tab. You can specify the number of pings or an unlimited number of pings until otherwise interrupted.

Lookup

The Lookup tab, shown in Figure 9.18, is a straightforward tool that provides both forward and reverse Domain Name System (DNS) lookups using an Internet domain name to find an IP address and an IP address to find an Internet domain name, respectively. Typically, when a lookup is successful, you will also be provided with DNS server information that is authoritative for that domain. To do a basic lookup, enter the domain name to be queried in the entry field adjacent to Please Enter An Internet Address To Lookup and then click the Lookup button. Although a number of advanced options are available within this tool, they are beyond the scope of the subject material tested on the Mac OS X Administration Basics exam.

Traceroute

The Trace Route tab, shown in Figure 9.19, can investigate the route/path between your computer and a specified Internet address. This is a useful tool in the investigation of various Internet performance issues.

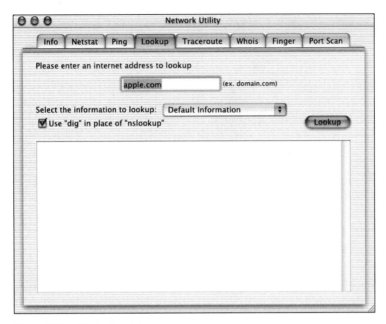

Figure 9.18   The Lookup tab.

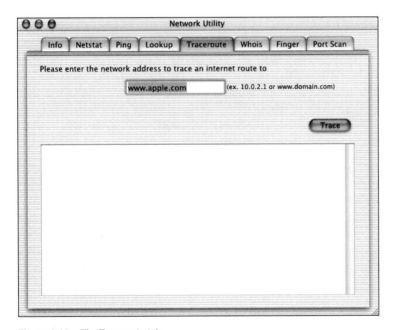

Figure 9.19   The Traceroute tab.

The Command Line

After years of being conditioned to use the Mac OS's world-class GUI, the command line is about as alien as it gets for longtime Mac devotees. I sometimes joke that the evolution of the OS interface has devolved us back to a Pleistocene period mentality of cave wall paintings. Well, Apple's here to tell you that the written word is not dead, at least when in reference to Mac OS X's command-line interface.

As an Apple Solution Expert (ASE), I have the privilege of attending a monthly meeting called the ASE Technical Kitchen. At these meetings, I learn about various Macintosh-related technologies, both Apple and third party in origin. To paraphrase one of the Apple technical representatives I encountered at these meetings, "99 percent of all administrative tasks are intended to be done through the Aqua GUI. If this is not the case, then Apple is not doing its job." I have also heard Apple representatives state that the command line is an optional element within Mac OS X, and it's there only if you want to use it. Although I honestly believe that this is Apple's true intention and that one day this might be the case, with the current state of Mac OS X utilities, it is almost impossible to completely negate the reality of the command line as a necessary utility.

Luckily, Apple realizes that there are a lot of us who may be a bit reluctant about using the command line, and Apple has taken this into account. For the Mac OS X Administration Basics exam, it is not necessary to do a cannonball or a belly flop into the proverbial command-line pool; rather, you can approach by wading in and testing its waters. For the exam, you will need to have more of a conceptual knowledge of using the command line over actual know-how. In the following subsections, I have put together a command-line essentials survival guide for the Mac OS X Administration Basics exam.

Command-Line Essentials

Simply stated, the command line provides a non-GUI way of interacting with Mac OS X. As stated previously, for day-to-day purposes the Aqua interface should be sufficient in providing the means to execute the majority of tasks necessary for the support and administration of Mac OS X. The command line is a result of Mac OS X's Unix underpinnings. The command line can be accessed via four different methods: logging in as ">console", remote login, single-user mode, and the Terminal application.

To enter the Console, you will first need to disable the "Automatically Log In" option and set the "Display Login Window As: Name And Password Entry Fields" option from within the Login Window tab of the Login preference pane. Next, you will need to log out and log back in. When presented with the Login window, type ">console" in the name field and click Login within the login window. This will circumvent the GUI and bring you into the command line. To exit out of the command line back to the GUI, simply type "exit" at the prompt and hit Return.

As mentioned in Chapter 7, remote login allows a local user account to remotely login by means of SSH. From this command line, commands can be entered as if the user were logged in locally on the system.

When engaged, single-user mode allows access to a majority of the Mac OS X file system as if you were the owner. Single-user mode is activated by holding down Command+S at system startup, and it is exited by simply typing "reboot" and hitting Return at the command prompt. A feature of single-user mode is that it disables multiuser processes and is typically used for troubleshooting purposes.

The Anatomy of the Command Prompt

The command prompt is where all of Mac OS X's Unix commands are entered. The command prompt also contains information such as the name of the machine, directory, and current user. All commands entered at the command prompt are followed by the Return key. Figure 9.20 depicts the command prompt.

Here's the breakdown of the designations for Figure 9.20:

➤ A is the machine name. The term *localhost* is the generic name of a machine linked to an IP address.

➤ B is the current directory. ~ is the command-line representation for a user's home folder.

➤ C is the current user. salitt is my short username.

fsck -y (Single-User Mode)

The file system check utility (**fsck**) is the command line equivalent to the Disk First Aid portion of the Disk Utility. It can be used as an alternative in the event that Mac OS X Install CD is unavailable. To use it, you will need to start the Macintosh in single-user mode. Type "**fsck –y**" at the # prompt and hit Return.

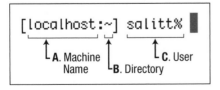

Figure 9.20   The command prompt.

The **fsck** utility will go through five phases of diagnostics and report the message "**** File System Was Modified ****" if anything was altered, repaired, or fixed. Without having to restart the system, repeat the **fsck –y** command until the message is no longer displayed. The "-y" portion of the **fsck –y** command's syntax is referred to as a *flag*. In this case, it's an affirmation of yes, which tells the **fsck** utility that you want it to repair all problems encountered without additional user intervention.

sudo

The **sudo** (super user do) command allows for the execution of commands as if you were logged in as the root user account. In fact, it is not necessary to enable the root user account to use the **sudo** command. Using the **sudo** command negates the need to log out and log back in as root to run certain commands. In order to use the **sudo** command, you will need to be an admin user.

man

The **man** (manual pages) command provides an online collection of reference manuals pages detailing just about every command that can be executed from the command prompt within Mac OS X.

pwd

The **pwd** (print working directory) command tells you where you are in the hierarchy of the directory structure by displaying the full path of the current working directory.

ls

The **ls** (list) command is somewhat similar to the MS-DOS command **dir**. The **ls** command will display an abbreviated list of all the contents of the current directory. By adding the flag -l (long list format), you can make the list include attributes of item type, permissions, link count, owner, group, size, date and time of last modification, and item name. The command-line syntax would read as follows: **ls –l**. Figure 9.21 depicts the **ls –l** command within Mac OS X's Terminal application.

chmod

The **chmod** (change mode) command offers similar functionality to the Privileges portion of the Show Info command from within the Finder. It can be used to change the definition of access privileges for a file or set of files.

chown

The **chown** command can be used to change ownership for a file or set of files.

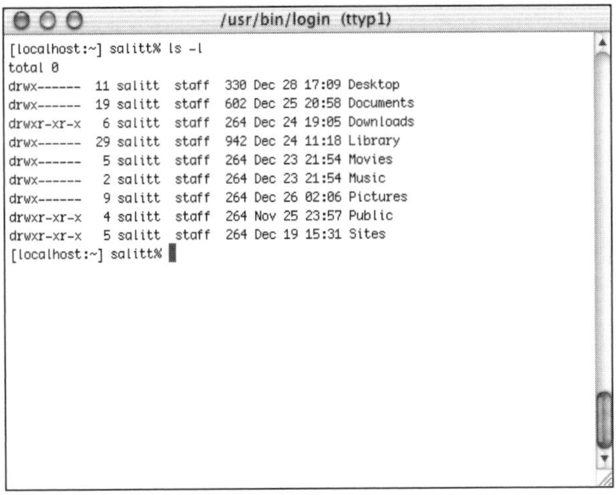

```
⊙ ○ ○              /usr/bin/login  (ttyp1)
[localhost:~] salitt% ls -l
total 0
drwx------  11 salitt  staff   330 Dec 28 17:09 Desktop
drwx------  19 salitt  staff   602 Dec 25 20:58 Documents
drwxr-xr-x   6 salitt  staff   264 Dec 24 19:05 Downloads
drwx------  29 salitt  staff   942 Dec 24 11:18 Library
drwx------   5 salitt  staff   264 Dec 23 21:54 Movies
drwx------   2 salitt  staff   264 Dec 23 21:54 Music
drwx------   9 salitt  staff   264 Dec 26 02:06 Pictures
drwxr-xr-x   4 salitt  staff   264 Nov 25 23:57 Public
drwxr-xr-x   5 salitt  staff   264 Dec 19 15:31 Sites
[localhost:~] salitt% █
```

Figure 9.21   The **ls –l** command as entered in the Terminal application.

Software Updates

The Software Update preference pane, shown in Figure 9.22, is Mac OS X's functional equivalent of OS 9's Software Update control panel. The Software Update preference pane offers a straightforward approach to obtaining system software updates for Mac OS X. The Software Update preference pane is accessed from within the System Preferences application and is only applicable to Mac OS X software updates. In order to update the Mac OS 9 portion of the Classic app, you will need to boot the computer from Mac OS 9 and run its Software Update control panel. Software updates can be scheduled as well as manually executed. One of the nicest features of the Software Update preference pane is the Show Log function. This provides an orderly account of all installed software updates via the Software Update preference pane. Lastly, as with all Mac OS X software installations, you will be required to supply an admin username and password before the installation can proceed.

Reinstallation

If you find that your Mac OS X system has become irreparably hosed, reinstallation may become necessary. It may be possible to reinstall Mac OS X without necessitating the reinitialization of the hard disk. This is dependent on the fact that since the initial release of Mac OS X, Apple has released a number of software updates. If your Mac OS X installer build is lagging several revisions behind the current iteration installed on your hard disk, it is important to carefully research the Apple Knowledge Base as to whether reinstallation is possible. Remember, if reinstallation over an existing installation is your intention, do *not* select the erase option.

Figure 9.22 Mac OS X's Software Update preference pane.

Ultimately, circumstances may require a complete wiping of the hard drive as well as a complete reinstallation and configuration of the OS. As of the completion of this book, there has been very little in the way of native backup software offerings for Mac OS X. The only commercially shipped product is TRI-EDRE Developments' Tri-BACKUP 3, which is also being sold FWB under the name BackUp ToolKit. If you do not have access to either of these utilities, you will minimally need to make a copy of all user folders and, if need be, any third-party applications to another volume. A quick way to copy off the user folders without getting tangled by Mac OS X's privileges is to make the copy while booted from Mac OS 9 because OS 9 does not recognize Mac OS X's security features. From my personal experience, I have found that it's possible to make restorable Finder copies of most OS X applications while booted in Mac OS X. However, even with this option available, I would not use this as a substitution in lieu of application reinstallation if the installers are available. Although it's beyond the scope of the exam, once the OS and the applications have been reinstalled, you will need to manually re-create all the user accounts. Finally, skillful reintegration of the contents of the copied user folders can soften the blow of a complete wipe and reinstallation.

As for Mac OS 9, it is possible to install and reinstall it within a Mac OS X–installed partition at any given time. First, do *not* use the Apple-provided software restore CDs. Second, if you are making any form of Mac OS 9 installation on an existing Mac OS X–installed volume, you will need to specify it as a clean installation from within the Mac OS 9 installer. This can be accomplished by clicking the Option button within the Mac OS 9 installer and placing a check in the box adjacent to the Clean Installation option. You will need to verify that you have the minimum required version of Mac OS 9 that is appropriate for the target computer system. As stated in Chapter 8, when you first start Classic, and depending on your iteration of Mac OS 9, a number of OS components are copied into the Mac OS 9 System Folder. Finally, if you had a previous installation of Mac OS 9, you will need to reintegrate any desired third-party system components.

Apple Troubleshooting Methodology

The Apple troubleshooting methodology is a progressive approach to problem solving. It starts off using passive troubleshooting techniques such as force-quitting a frozen application and relaunching it. Then it involves power-cycling the computer as well as conducting research for known issues in the AppleCare Knowledge Base. These tactics are examples of what are called *innocuous fixes*. If the problem is still unresolved, the troubleshooter might employ more aggressive techniques, such as running Repair Disk, zapping the PRAM (Command+ Option+P+R, used at system restart), and applying applicable software and firmware updates. These types of fixes are know as *invasive*, because they may have a more profound impact on the overall condition of the system and might result in other repercussions. Finally, we have what are known as *drastic measures*. They are typified by such tactics as reinstalling applications and system software, and as a last resort, formatting the hard disk and starting over. Having a good game plan is just as important as knowing your stuff. As for me, my personal philosophy is: it is not what you know as much as it is the methodology of how you employ your talent.

Split-Half Search

Split-half search is a strategy of troubleshooting that dates back to very beginnings of Macintosh computing. Split-half search is a process of elimination. In Macintosh desktop operating systems that predated Mac OS X, the split-half strategy was typically used in searches to eliminate extension conflicts that caused machines to crash during system startup. Within Mac OS X, the split-half strategy can still be applied as an effective troubleshooting tool in many ways. Not only will it work within the Classic Application environment, but it can also be applied in any situation that can be troubleshot by means of the process of elimination. For instance, let's say you have an application crashing on startup. The split-half strategy could be applied by trying to launch the offending application from within another user account. If the program successfully launches, it might be possible to eliminate damaged software as an issue and focus on other potential causes, such as corrupt preferences or software conflicts.

 Throughout this book, I reference the AppleCare Knowledge Base. Be aware that the article names change from time to time, but the Article IDs should remain the same.

Practice Questions

Question 1

> True or false: An application can be force-quit from the Console application.
>
> ○ a. True
>
> ○ b. False

The correct answer is b. It is not possible to force-quite an application from the Console. The Console is an information-gathering tool that displays the Mac OS X system.log as entries are being written to it.

Question 2

> When is it possible to install Mac OS 9 on a Mac OS X system?
>
> ○ a. Before Mac OS X is installed
>
> ○ b. After Mac OS X is installed
>
> ○ c. After Mac OS X is installed, but only on a separate partition
>
> ○ d. Anytime

The correct answer is d. It is possible to install and reinstall Mac OS 9 within a Mac OS X–installed partition at any given time. Although answers a, b, and c are technically correct, they are only components of answer d, which is the best answer in this case. Therefore, answers a, b, and c are incorrect answers.

Question 3

When using the command line, what is the command to change the access privileges of a file?

○ a. **pwd**

○ b. **chown**

○ c. **man**

○ d. **chmod**

The correct answer is d. The **chmod** command can be used to change the definition of access privileges for a file or set of files. Answer a is incorrect because the **pwd** command tells you where you are in the hierarchy of the directory structure by displaying the full path of the current working directory. Answer b is incorrect because the **chown** command is used to change ownership for a file or set of files. Answer c is incorrect because the **man** (manual pages) command provides an online collection of reference manuals pages detailing just about every command that can be executed from the command prompt within Mac OS X.

Question 4

True or false: It is possible to force-quit individual applications within Classic.

○ a. True

○ b. False

The correct answer is b. You cannot force-quit individual Classic applications, although you can force-quit the entire Classic Application environment.

Question 5

> Which one of the following commands cannot be used with the Terminal application?
>
> ○ a. **top**
>
> ○ b. **sudo**
>
> ○ c. **ls**
>
> ○ d. **pwd**
>
> ○ e. **man**
>
> ○ f. None of the above
>
> ○ g. All of the above

The correct answer is f. I worded this question this way to illustrate that it is important to carefully read what each question is asking, even if it is poorly worded. All the commands listed can be used with Mac OS X's Terminal application. Answers a, b, c, d, and e are all valid commands for the Terminal application. The **top** command provides a detailed view of processor usage within the command line. The **sudo** command allows for the execution of commands within the Terminal application, as if you were logged in as the root user while you're really logged in as a normal user. The **ls** command displays an abbreviated list of all the contents of the current directory. The **pwd** command displays the full path of the current working directory, and the **man** command provides an online collection of reference manuals pages detailing just about every command that can be executed from the command prompt within Mac OS X. Therefore, answers a, b, c, d, and e are incorrect. Answer g is incorrect for the same reasons.

Question 6

> What is the key combination that will activate verbose mode at startup?
>
> ○ a. Option+V
>
> ○ b. Shift+Option+V
>
> ○ c. Command+V
>
> ○ d. Shift+Command+V
>
> ○ e. None of the above

The correct answer is c. The key combination of Command+V will activate verbose mode at startup. Answer a is incorrect because the key combination of Option+V does nothing. Answer b is incorrect because the key combination of Shift+Option+V does nothing. Answer d is incorrect because the key combination of Shift+Command+V does nothing. Answer e is incorrect for all these reasons.

Question 7

> When using the command line, what is the command to change ownership of a file?
>
> ○ a. **pwd**
>
> ○ b. **chown**
>
> ○ c. **man**
>
> ○ d. **chmod**

The correct answer is b. The **chown** command can be used to change ownership for a file or set of files. Answer a is incorrect because the **pwd** command tells you where you are in the hierarchy of the directory structure by displaying the full path of the current working directory. Answer c is incorrect because the **man** (manual pages) command provides an online collection of reference manuals pages detailing just about every command that can be executed from the command prompt within Mac OS X. Answer d is incorrect because the **chmod** command is used to change the definition of access privileges for a file or set of files.

Question 8

> What is the command required to enter commands within the Terminal as the root account user while logged in as a normal user?
>
> ○ a. **sudo**
>
> ○ b. **top**
>
> ○ c. **man**
>
> ○ d. **lsd**

The correct answer is a. The **sudo** command allows for the execution of commands within the Terminal application as if you were logged in as the root user account when you're really logged in as a normal user. Answer b is incorrect because the **top** command provides a detailed view of processor usage within the command line. Answer c is incorrect because the **man** command provides an online collection of reference manuals pages detailing just about every command that can be executed from the command prompt within Mac OS X. Answer d is incorrect because **lsd** is a powerful psychedelic drug that produces temporary hallucinations and a schizophrenic psychotic state.

Question 9

> Your Macintosh has become nonresponsive and a series of white text on a black background has appeared on the screen. What has occurred?
>
> ○ a. A ping
>
> ○ b. A traceroute
>
> ○ c. A force quit
>
> ○ d. A kernel panic

The correct answer is d. When the microkernel encounters a situation that it cannot handle, a kernel panic occurs. Typically, the Macintosh will become nonresponsive and a series of white text on a black background will be drawn on top what ever is being viewed on the monitor at the time of the occurrence. Answer a is incorrect because ping is a network diagnostic tool that can be used to validate the connectivity of another IP-aware networking device on the Internet. Answer b is incorrect because traceroute is a network diagnostic tool that can be used to investigate the route/path between your computer and a specified Internet address. Answer c is incorrect because a force quit is a way to terminate a single unresponsive application without having to restart the computer.

Need to Know More?

 The Apple Knowledge Base is the definite resource for researching Apple technical support issues. It can be found at **http://kbase.info.apple.com/**.

Check out Article ID 58477, titled "Macintosh: How to Use Startup Manager to Select a Startup Volume."

Check out Article ID 75187, titled "Mac OS X: Software Installations Require Administrator Password."

Check out Article ID 88279, titled "Mac OS X 10.1: Cannot Install Mac OS X 10.1.X Update."

Check out Article ID 106178, titled "Mac OS X 10.0: Startup Manager Only Displays One Operating System per Volume."

Check out Article ID 106214, titled "Mac OS X: Why, When, and How to Run fsck for File System Maintenance."

Check out Article ID 106215, titled "Mac OS X 10.0: File System Dirty, Run fsck."

Check out Article ID 106227, titled "Mac OS X 10.0: What Is a Kernel Panic?"

Check out Article ID 106228, titled "Mac OS X 10.0: How to Log a Kernel Panic."

Check out Article ID 106270, titled "Mac OS X 10.0: Disk Utility Incorrectly Reports Disk Errors on Startup Volume."

Check out Article ID 106294, titled "Mac OS X 10.0: How to Reinstall Mac OS 9 or Recover from a Software Restore."

Check out Article ID 106392, titled "Mac OS X: How to Troubleshoot a Software Update Installation."

Check out Article ID 106464, titled "Mac OS X: Troubleshooting a Startup Issue."

Check out Article ID 106482, titled "Mac OS X 10.1: How to Set up Open Firmware Password Protection."

Check out Article ID 106514, titled "Mac OS X: Start Up from CD-ROM to Reformat Any Volume on Startup Device Between Mac OS (HFS) and Unix (UFS) Disk Formats."

Check out Article ID 106527, titled "Mac OS X 10.1: Some Preference Lost After Using 10.1 Upgrade CD."

Check out Article ID 106594, titled "Mac OS X 10.1: Mac OS X Server 10.1: How to Use Apple-Supplied RAID Software."

Check out Article ID 106634, titled "Mac OS X Update 10.1.2: Enhancements and 'Before You Install' Information."

Check out Article ID 106171, titled "Mac OS X: Double-Clicking a File Opens the Wrong Application."

Check out Article ID 120095, titled "Open Firmware Password 1.0.2: Information and Download."

Sample Test

In this chapter, we will review the structure of the Apple Mac OS X Administration Basics Exam (9L0-500) and some tactics to help you develop a successful test-taking strategy, including how to choose proper answers, how to decode ambiguity, how to work within the Prometric testing framework, how to decide what you need to memorize, and how to prepare for the test. At the end of the chapter, I include 80 questions on subject material pertinent to the test. In Chapter 11, you'll find the answer key to this test.

Questions, Questions, Questions

There should be no doubt in your mind that you are facing a test full of specific and pointed questions. The exam that you take is of a fixed length; it will include 85 questions, and you will be allotted a time limit of 90 minutes. The exam essentially consists of 80 questions (five questions located at the beginning of the exam are of statistical/demographic nature). Some examples of such questions are: How did you study for this exam? What is your job function? The computer maintains an onscreen counter/clock so that you can check the time remaining any time you like.

Note: The passing score for the Mac OS X Administration Basics Exam is 75 percent. You must get 60 questions correct out of 80 total questions.

All exam questions will belong to one of four basic types:

➤ Multiple choice with a single answer

➤ Multiple choice with multiple answers

➤ Fill-in-the-blank with a single answer

➤ True or false

You should always take the time to read a question at least twice before selecting an answer, and you should always look for an Exhibit button as you examine each question. Exhibits include graphical information related to the questions. An exhibit is usually a screen capture of program output or GUI information that you must examine to analyze the question's contents and formulate an answer. The Exhibit button displays graphics and visual aids used to help explain a question, provide additional data, or illustrate program behavior.

Not every question has only one answer; many questions require multiple answers. Therefore, you should read each question carefully, determine how many answers are necessary or possible, and look for additional hints or instructions when selecting answers. Such instructions often appear in brackets immediately following the questions themselves (for multiple-answer questions).

Picking Proper Answers

Obviously, the only way to pass any exam is to select enough of the right answers to obtain a passing score. However, the Mac OS X Administration Basics Exam (9L0-500) is not standardized like the SAT and GRE exams; it's far more diabolical and convoluted. In some cases, questions are ambiguous and strangely worded, and deciphering them can be a real challenge. In those cases, your answer may need to rely on a process of elimination. Almost always, at least one answer out of the possible choices for a question can be eliminated immediately because it matches one of these conditions:

➤ The answer is not applicable to the question.

➤ The answer describes a nonexistent issue, an invalid option, or an imaginary state.

➤ The answer may be eliminated because of content provided within the question itself.

After you eliminate all answers that are obviously wrong, you can apply your retained knowledge to eliminate further incorrect answers. Look for items that sound correct but refer to actions, commands, or features that are not present or not available in the situation that the question describes.

If you're still faced with a blind guess among two or more potentially correct answers, *reread* the question. Try to picture how each of the possible remaining answers would apply to the situation. *Be especially sensitive to terminology.* Sometimes the choice of words ("remove" instead of "disable") can make the difference between a right answer and a wrong one.

Only when time is running out, and you've completely exhausted your ability to eliminate incorrect answers and continue to remain stumped about which of the remaining answers is correct, should you guess at an answer. *An unanswered question offers you no points and counts against you, but guessing gives you at least some possibility of getting a question right.* Guessing should only be used as a last resort.

Decoding Ambiguity

Technology certification exams have a reputation for including questions that can be difficult to interpret and are confusing or ambiguous.

Questions often give away their answers, and you might have to use the sleuthing powers of Dixon Hill to see the clues. Often, subtle hints appear in the question's text in such a way that they seem almost irrelevant to the situation. You must realize that each question is a test unto itself and that you need to inspect and successfully navigate each question to pass the exam. Look for small clues, such as the mention of when the event takes place, exact terminology, privileges, as well as configurations and settings. Little things such as these can point to the right answer if they're *properly* understood; if missed, they can leave you facing a blind guess.

Another common difficulty with certification exams is terminology. Be sure to brush up on the key terms presented at the beginning of each chapter and read the glossary at the end of this book *the day before* you take the test.

Working within the Framework

The test questions appear in random order, and many elements or issues that are mentioned in one question may crop up in another question. It's not uncommon to find that an incorrect answer to one question is the correct answer to another question, or vice versa. Take the time to read *every* answer to each question, even if you recognize the correct answer to a question immediately. That extra reading may spark a memory or remind you about a feature or function that helps you on another question elsewhere in the exam.

Because you are taking a fixed-length test, you can revisit any question as many times as you like. If you're uncertain of the answer to a question, check the box that's provided to mark it for easy return later on. You should also mark questions that you think may offer information you can use to answer other questions. When I took the exam, I marked somewhere between 25 and 50 percent of the questions. The testing software is designed to let you mark every question if you choose; use this framework to your advantage. Everything you'll want to see again should be marked; the testing software can then help you return to marked questions quickly and easily.

I strongly recommend that you first read the entire test quickly before getting caught up in answering individual questions. Doing this will help to jog your memory as you review the potential answers and can help you identify questions that you want to mark for easy access to their contents. You can also identify and mark the tricky questions for easy return. The key is to make a quick pass over the exam, survey the terrain (to know what you're up against), and then work it thoroughly on a second pass, when you can begin to answer all questions systematically and consistently.

The Prometric testing center will provide you with a pen or pencil and a blank sheet of paper or, in some cases, an erasable plastic sheet with an erasable felt-tip pen. You're allowed to write down any information you want on this sheet. If you see something in a question or in one of the answers that jogs your memory on a topic, write it down on your piece of paper. Sometimes, what you record from one question can help you on other questions later on.

Deciding What to Memorize

The amount of memorization you must undertake for an exam depends on how well you remember what you've read and how well you know the Mac OS X by heart. If you're a visual thinker and can see the drop-down menus and dialog boxes in your head, you won't need to memorize as much as someone who's less visually oriented. However, the exam will stretch your abilities to recollect the features and functions, as well as support and maintenance approaches, of Mac OS X.

At a minimum, you'll want to know the following kinds of information:

➤ Installation and interface

➤ User accounts

➤ File system

➤ Application support

➤ Classic support

➤ Networking

➤ File sharing

➤ Device support

➤ Administrative functions

➤ Command line

➤ Problem solving

If you work your way through this book while sitting at a machine with Mac OS X installed, you should have little or no difficulty when exam time comes. Also, don't forget that The Cram Sheet at the front of the book is designed to capture the material that's most important to memorize; use this to guide your studies as well.

Preparing for the Test

The best way to prepare for the test—after you've studied—is to take at least one practice exam. I've included one here in this chapter for that reason; the test questions are located in the pages that follow. (Unlike the questions in the preceding chapters in this book, the answers don't follow the questions immediately; you'll have to flip to Chapter 11 to review the answers separately.)

Give yourself 90 minutes to take the exam, and keep yourself on the honor system—don't look at earlier text in the book or jump ahead to the answer key. When your time is up or you've finished the questions, you can check your work in Chapter 11. Pay special attention to the explanations for the incorrect answers; these can also help to reinforce your knowledge of the material. Knowing how to recognize correct answers is good, but understanding why incorrect answers are wrong can be equally valuable.

Taking the Test

Relax. Once you're sitting in front of the testing computer, there's nothing more you can do to increase your knowledge or preparation. Take a deep breath, stretch, and start reading that first question.

You don't need to rush, either. If you have studied, you will have plenty of time to complete each question, and because you are taking a fixed-length test, if you encounter a question and you are clueless, you can mark it for later return. Both easy and difficult questions are intermixed throughout the test in random order. Don't cheat yourself by spending too much time on a hard question early in the test, thereby depriving yourself of the time you need to answer the questions at the end of the test. In fact, don't spend more than a minute on any single question. If it takes you any longer, mark it for later return. On a fixed-length test, you can go through the entire test, and, before returning to marked questions for a second visit, you can figure out how much time you have remaining per question. As you answer each question, remove its mark. Continue to review the remaining marked questions until you run out of time or complete the test. In fact, if time is running out and you still have questions that stump you, take an educated guess and move on.

That about wraps it up. Here are some questions for you to practice on. Good luck!

Question 1

Which of the following is not a port?

○ a. Ethernet

○ b. Proxy

○ c. AirPort

○ d. Modem

Question 2

What types of applications can run in both MAC OS X and MAC OS 9 natively?

○ a. Classic

○ b. Carbon

○ c. Cocoa

○ d. All of the above

Question 3

True or false: There is no difference between a package and a bundle.

○ a. True

○ b. False

Question 4

LDAP and NetInfo are examples of what?

○ a. Protocols

○ b. Ports

○ c. Proxies

○ d. Directory services

Question 5

What is the name of the folder for sharing files among local user accounts?

○ a. Public

○ b. Users

○ c. Shared

○ d. Drop Box

Question 6

True or false: There is no difference between the root account and an admin user account.

○ a. True

○ b. False

Question 7

What is the name of the software used to select printers in the Classic application environment?

○ a. Desktop Printing

○ b. Print Center

○ c. Chooser

○ d. Printer Utility

Question 8

What is the name of the OS X software that is used to select OS 9 as a startup system on a single-partition system?

○ a. Startup Manager

○ b. OS Picker

○ c. Startup Disk control panel

○ d. Startup Disk preference pane

Question 9

> True or false: The Apple Menu is customizable in Mac OS X.
>
> ○ a. True
>
> ○ b. False

Question 10

> Which of the following is a not a limitation of peer-to-peer file sharing under Mac OS X?
>
> ○ a. Does not natively support Windows clients
>
> ○ b. Has preset user access points
>
> ○ c. Only supports 10 simultaneous users
>
> ○ d. All of the above
>
> ○ e. None of the above

Question 11

> How are AFP servers accessed within Mac OS X?
>
> ○ a. Through the Chooser
>
> ○ b. Through the Finder
>
> ○ c. Through the Network Utility
>
> ○ d. Through Directory Setup

Question 12

> True or false: Mac OS 9 supports Mac OS X's security model.
>
> ○ a. True
>
> ○ b. False

Question 13

True or false: Mac OS X can serve Web pages.

○ a. True

○ b. False

Question 14

Where within the GUI would one enable the root account?

○ a. Directory Setup

○ b. Console

○ c. NetInfo Manager

○ d. Users preference pane

Question 15

MAC OS 9 legacy applications are referred to as _____ ?

○ a. Standard applications

○ b. Carbon applications

○ c. Classic applications

○ d. Packages

Question 16

What is the name of Apple's multimedia engine?

○ a. QuickTime

○ b. OpenGL

○ c. Quartz

○ d. PDF

Question 17

True or false: An admin user can reset the password of another admin user.

○ a.   True

○ b.   False

Question 18

What is the name of the Aqua GUI element that can be customized to hold frequently accessed applications?

○ a.   Apple Menu

○ b.   Pop-up menu

○ c.   Dock

○ d.   Start Menu

Question 19

Where is DHCP configured in Mac OS X?

○ a.   The Network Utility

○ b.   The Internet preference pane

○ c.   Console

○ d.   The Network preference pane

Question 20

True or false: The AppleTalk control panel retains functionality within the Classic application environment.

○ a.   True

○ b.   False

Question 21

Which of the following are considered features of a modern OS? [Check all correct answers]

❑ a. Preemptive multitasking

❑ b. Protected memory

❑ c. Cooperative multitasking

❑ d. Symmetric multiprocessing

Question 22

Which of the following are supported servers for Mac OS X's Mail application?

○ a. POP

○ b. IMAP

○ c. Unix

○ d. iTools

○ e. All of the above

Question 23

Where would one add an additional user for FTP access within Mac OS X?

○ a. The Network preference pane

○ b. The Users preference pane

○ c. The Login preference pane

○ d. The Internet preference pane

Question 24

What piece of software is used to configure TCP/IP for the Classic environment?

○ a. The Network Utility

○ b. The Network preference pane

○ c. The Internet preference pane

○ d. The TCP/IP control panel

Question 25

What is the name of the technology that allows Mac OS X to utilize dual-processor systems?

○ a. The Classic Application environment

○ b. Symmetric multiprocessing

○ c. Cooperative multitasking

○ d. Preemptive multitasking

Question 26

In terms of Mac OS X, Mach refers to what?

○ a. The speed of processing

○ b. A native OS X application

○ c. A synonym for the command line

○ d. The foundation that provides basic services for all other parts of the operating system

Question 27

True or false: Mac OS X has built-in support for AppleTalk printing.

○ a. True

○ b. False

Question 28

When you're examining file privileges via the command line, what would the following mean?

rw-r--r--

○ a. Everyone has Read privileges

○ b. The group has Read privileges

○ c. The owner has Read & Write privileges

○ d. All of the above

Question 29

What is the tool that is used to verify the TCP/IP connectivity of another IP-enabled networking device?

○ a. Ping

○ b. Directory Setup

○ c. Console

○ d. Apple System Profiler

Question 30

What is the Apple designation for MAC OS X's new GUI?

○ a. Classic

○ b. Aqua

○ c. Platinum

○ d. Luna

Question 31

True or false: Open Type is a native font format of Mac OS X.

○ a. True

○ b. False

Question 32

True or false: It is possible to configure AppleTalk and TCP/IP on the same port.

○ a. True

○ b. False

Question 33

Which of the following are natively supported directory services in Mac OS X? [Check all correct answers]

❑ a. LDAPv2

❑ b. Windows Active Directory

❑ c. NDS eDirectory

❑ d. NetInfo

Question 34

What would you use to configure printer connectivity in Mac OS X?

○ a. The Print Center

○ b. Desktop Printing

○ c. The Chooser

○ d. The Printer Utility

Question 35

What is an alternative name for the TrueBlueEnvironment?

○ a. Carbon

○ b. Java

○ c. Cocoa

○ d. Classic

Question 36

True or false: When you're deleting a user account, the deleted user's files can be transferred to any user.

○ a. True

○ b. False

Question 37

What is the key combination to start using verbose mode?

○ a. Option+V

○ b. Shift+Option+V

○ c. Shift+Command+V

○ d. Command+V

Question 38

LPR printing allows Mac OS X to print using what network protocol?

○ a. TCP/IP

○ b. AppleTalk

○ c. PPP

○ d. PPPoE

Question 39

What is the name of the software used to configure access to directory services in Mac OS X?

○ a. The Internet preference pane

○ b. Directory Setup

○ c. Network Utility

○ d. The Network preference pane

Question 40

What is the Apple recommended workaround for a printer that is not supported in Mac OS X?

○ a. Go buy a new printer

○ b. Email the document instead of printing

○ c. Skip printing and go have a beer

○ d. Save the document as a PDF and print from Mac OS 9

Question 41

True or false: An alias is the OS 9 equivalent of a symbolic link.

○ a. True

○ b. False

Question 42

A _____ is a single point of reference for a set of configura-tions for networking ports and protocols.

○ a. Proxy

○ b. Directory Service

○ c. Location

○ d. Setup Assistant

Question 43

Which of the following is a function of protected memory?

○ a. It isolates applications in their individual memory workspaces.

○ b. It provides support for multiprocessor Macintosh computer systems.

○ c. It prioritizes processor tasks by order of importance.

○ d. None of the above.

Question 44

What is the command that displays processor activity within the Terminal application?

○ a. **ls**

○ b. **ls -l**

○ c. **sudo**

○ d. **top**

Question 45

Which are valid ways to repair a hard disk in Mac OS X? [Check all correct answers]

- ❏ a. Reboot into single-user mode and use **fsck-y** at the command prompt.

- ❏ b. Open the Terminal application and use **fsck-y** at the command prompt.

- ❏ c. Run Disk Utility off of the hard disk.

- ❏ d. Reboot off of the Mac OS X Installer CD and select Repair Disk from the menu bar.

Question 46

True or false: MAC OS 9 control panels have a global effect within MAC OS X.

- ○ a. True

- ○ b. False

Question 47

What are some benefits of the Mach 3.0 microkernel? [Check all correct answers]

- ❏ a. Preemptive multitasking

- ❏ b. Protected memory

- ❏ c. Cooperative multitasking

- ❏ d. Symmetric multiprocessing

Question 48

What is the difference between the root account and the superuser account?

- ○ a. The former has more privileges than the latter.

- ○ b. The latter has more privileges than the former.

- ○ c. The root account exists by default, but you have to create the superuser account.

- ○ d. There is no difference.

Question 49

True or false: It is possible to navigate to invisible items through the Aqua interface.

○ a. True

○ b. False

Question 50

What might be an advantage of installing Mac OS X on separate partitions?

○ a. It's the quickest way to install Mac OS X.

○ b. It provides a safety net in the event that the OS X portion becomes damaged.

○ c. There is no advantage.

○ d. Answers a and b are both correct.

Question 51

True or false: A Mac OS 9 machine can be an AFP file-sharing client of a Mac OS X machine.

○ a. True

○ b. False

Question 52

What is the preferred format for a MAC OS X volume?

○ a. UFS

○ b. HFS+

○ c. NFS

○ d. HFS

Question 53

In terms of Mac OS X, what does Darwin refer to?

○ a. An Open Source community/Apple joint project

○ b. A cross-platform multimedia authoring and distribution engine

○ c. An annoying dolphin from a defunct television program

○ d. A standard graphics application programming interface (API) through which software and hardware manufacturers can build 3D applications and hardware across multiple platforms on a common standard

Question 54

What is the command you would enter in the Terminal to view Mac OS X's built-in reference documentation?

○ a. **chmod**

○ b. **ls**

○ c. **man**

○ d. **chown**

Question 55

True or false: Using the Startup Manager is a valid way to pick among multiple OS installations on the same partition.

○ a. True

○ b. False

Question 56

Which of the following are methods Apple recommends for recording the contents displayed by a kernel panic? [Check all correct answers]

❑ a. Use the Grab application.

❑ b. Use verbose mode.

❑ c. Print it.

❑ d. Use a digital camera.

❑ e. Use pen and paper.

Question 57

True or false: It is possible to have multiple installations of MAC OS 9 on the same partition as MAC OS X.

○ a. True

○ b. False

Question 58

True or false: MAC OS X is a multiuser operating system.

○ a. True

○ b. False

Question 59

AppleTalk and TCP/IP are examples of what?

○ a. Protocols

○ b. Ports

○ c. Proxies

○ d. Topologies

Question 60

Which of the following is a true statement about a UFS formatted partition?

○ a. It does not support the operation of Classic application environment.

○ b. It does not support AirPort.

○ c. It is not case preserving.

○ d. It is unsupported in Mac OS X.

Question 61

True or false: When using the ProcessViewer application, it is possible to kill processes that are not owned by the logged-in user.

○ a. True

○ b. False

Question 62

What is the Mac OS X functional equivalent to Mac OS 9's Startup Items?

○ a. Login Items

○ b. Panes

○ c. Sheets

○ d. System Preferences

Question 63

What is the maximum number of groups an item can belong to?

○ a. Zero

○ b. One

○ c. Two

○ d. No limit

Question 64

True or false: Language preferences can be configured for a specific application.

○ a. True

○ b. False

Question 65

What is a search path?

○ a. It is a service that resolves domain names to IP addresses, and vice versa.

○ b. It is a hierarchically ordered acquisition of system resources.

○ c. It is a method of organizing data on storage media.

○ d. It is a control mechanism for user access to files, folders, and applications within Mac OS X.

Question 66

What is the name of the program that formats and partitions hard disks in Mac OS X?

○ a. Drive Setup

○ b. Disk Utility

○ c. Disk First Aid

○ d. Directory Setup

Question 67

Where do you locally store a font in OS X that is to be accessed globally throughout the entire system? [Check all correct answers]

❏ a. ~/Library/Fonts

❏ b. / Library/Fonts

❏ c. /System/Library/Fonts

❏ d. Mac OS 9 Fonts folder

Question 68

What folder does ~ represent within the command line?

○ a. Home

○ b. System

○ c. Fonts

○ d. Applications

Question 69

What is the Mac OS 9 equivalent of a Mac OS X framework?

○ a. CDEVs

○ b. Open Transport

○ c. Shared libraries

○ d. There is no equivalent

Question 70

What is the name of MAC OS X's 2D rendering technology?

○ a. Quiktime

○ b. OpenGL

○ c. QuickDraw

○ d. Quartz

Question 71

Which of the following are ways to terminate an unresponsive application within MAC OS X? [Check all correct answers]

❑ a. Use the **top** command in the Terminal.

❑ b. Force-quit the process through the ProcessViewer application.

❑ c. Use the **Force Quit** command located under the Apple Menu.

❑ d. Use the key combination Option+Command+Esc.

Question 72

What is the name of the folder that users can place their files into in order to share them with others over a network?

○ a. Public

○ b. Users

○ c. Shared

○ d. Drop Box

Question 73

Which of the following is not an option that can be configured within the login window? [Check all correct answers]

❑ a. Login Items

❑ b. New User Accounts

❑ c. Passwords

❑ d. Disable Restart and Shut Down buttons

Question 74

Which of the following are ways to access the command line? [Check all correct answers]

❑ a. Verbose

❑ b. >console

❑ c. Terminal

❑ d. Remote SSH

Question 75

True or false: Desktop Printing is a Mac OS X compatible technology.

○ a. True

○ b. False

Question 76

True or false: PPPoE can be configured for an analog modem.

O a. True

O b. False

Question 77

What is the minimum version of OS 9 required for the Classic application environment?

O a. 9.0

O b. 9.04

O c. 9.1

O d. 9.2

Question 78

True or false: Mac OS X requires a reboot after an external USB hard disk is plugged in.

O a. True

O b. False

Question 79

User accounts are administered through which of the following preference panes?

O a. Sharing

O b. Login

O c. Users

O d. Networking

Question 80

What is a negative ramification if the BSD Subsystem is not included in the MAC OS X installation?

○ a. FireWire devices will not function.

○ b. Network Printing will not function.

○ c. Multiple user accounts are unsupported.

○ d. There are no negative ramifications.

Answer Key

1. b	21. a, b, d	41. b	61. b
2. b	22. e	42. c	62. a
3. a	23. b	43. a	63. b
4. d	24. b	44. d	64. a
5. c	25. b	45. a, d	65. b
6. b	26. d	46. b	66. b
7. c	27. a	47. a, b, d	67. b, d
8. d	28. d	48. d	68. a
9. b	29. a	49. a	69. c
10. e	30. b	50. b	70. d
11. b	31. a	51. a	71. b, c, d
12. b	32. a	52. b	72. a
13. a	33. a, d	53. a	73. a, b, c, d
14. c	34. a	54. c	74. b, c, d
15. c	35. d	55. b	75. b
16. a	36. b	56. d, e	76. b
17. a	37. d	57. a	77. c
18. c	38. a	58. a	78. b
19. d	39. b	59. a	79. c
20. a	40. d	60. b	80. b

Question 1

Answer b is correct. A proxy is not a port. In terms of Mac OS X, proxies are a configuration of the Network preference pane. The Proxies tab provides OS X the facility to utilize a server as an intermediary conduit between a user's workstation and the Internet. When a request is made for Internet content, the request is passed along to the proxy server. The proxy server will then act on behalf of the client and forward the request on to the Internet, and it will relate the retrieved response back to the user. Answers a, c, and d are incorrect. Ethernet, AirPort, and Modem are all ports. A port, as referred to within the Network Preference Pane, is some form of physical connection to a data network.

Question 2

Answer b is correct. Carbonized applications can run *natively* in either Mac OS 9 or OS X. When running within OS X, Carbon applications take advantage of most of OS X's modern OS features, including the Aqua interface. In order for Carbon applications to run within Mac OS 9, the CarbonLib library must be present within the Extensions folder inside the Mac OS 9 System Folder. Answer a is incorrect. Classic applications run natively in Mac OS 9, but they require OS X's Classic application compatibility environment to run under Mac OS X. This allows OS X to run most Macintosh legacy applications that have not been updated to run natively. Answer c is incorrect. Although Cocoa applications run natively in Mac OS X, they are incompatible for Mac OS 9. Answer d is incorrect as a result of answer b.

Question 3

Answer a is correct. It is true that there is no difference between a package and a bundle. They are synonyms. A package/bundle is a single icon point-and-click representation of an application. Just like previous Classic applications, Mac OS X's Carbon and Cocoa applications can be composed of multiple subordinate files and resources. In the GUI, all these subordinate pieces are neatly wrapped up into a representation of a single executable file for the end user.

Question 4

Answer d is correct. LDAP and NetInfo are both examples of directory services. Directory services provide a consolidated user list that can be shared among multiple network services or servers for authentication. Directory services do not provide the services themselves, but rather describe how they are set up. Answer a is incorrect. A protocol is a set of rules for the exchange of data between computer systems. Answer b is incorrect. A port is some form of physical connection to a data network. Answer c is incorrect. A proxy is an intermediary conduit between a user's workstation and the Internet.

Question 5

Answer c is correct. The Shared folder is the place where local user accounts can share files among themselves locally on the system. Answer a is incorrect. The Public folder is the location of contents to be shared over a network. Answer b is incorrect. The Users folder is the parent directory for all Home folders for local user accounts. Answer d is incorrect. The Drop Box folder provides a safe haven for remotely connected users to place contents on the machine in a secure manner without the prying eyes of other connected users.

Question 6

Answer b is correct. There is a distinct difference between the root account and an admin user account. The root account has complete access to all settings and files within the operating system. The admin account has enough power to get the majority of the system administration tasks done without the potential liabilities associated with the root account.

Question 7

Answer c is correct. The Chooser is the software that is used to select printers in the Classic application environment. Answer a is incorrect. Desktop Printing is an unsupported technology in the Classic application environment. Answer b is incorrect. The Print Center is the software that allows Mac OS X to select printers. Answer d is incorrect. The Printer Utility is a Mac OS 9 application that is used to configure the hardware options in Apple manufactured printers.

Question 8

Answer d is correct. The Startup Disk preferences pane is the Mac OS X software that is used to select OS 9 as a startup OS on a single partition system. Answers a and b are incorrect. The Startup Manager, which is sometimes referred to as the OS Picker, is not a valid method of selecting a startup system on a partition that contains multiple operating systems. Answer c is incorrect. The Startup Disk control panel is the Mac OS 9 equivalent of OS X's Startup Disk preferences pane and has no functionality within Mac OS X.

Question 9

Answer b is correct. The Apple Menu in Mac OS X is not customizable.

Question 10

Answer e is correct. The answer is none of the above. Answers a, b, and c are all limitations of peer-to-peer file sharing. This is to distinguish Mac OS X product from Mac OS X server product for marketability. Answer d is incorrect as a result of answer e.

Question 11

Answer b is correct. AFP servers are accessed through Mac OS X's Finder. To connect to a server, simply select Connect to Server (Command+K) from the Go menu and you will be presented with a network service navigation window similar in functionality to that of Mac OS 9's Network Browser. Answer a is incorrect. The Chooser is one of Mac OS 9's mechanisms for accessing AFP servers. Answer c is incorrect. The Network Utility is a set of Mac OS X diagnostic tools for troubleshooting networking issues. Answer d is incorrect. The Directory Setup application is the program for configuring access to directory services in Mac OS X.

Question 12

Answer b is correct. Mac OS 9 does not support Mac OS X's security features.

Question 13

Answer a is correct. Mac OS X can serve Web pages. Mac OS X uses Apache as its Web server. Apache is an Open Source licensed Web server that is the Web-serving engine of Mac OS X.

Question 14

Answer c is correct. Within the GUI, the root account is enabled through the NetInfo Manager. Answer a is incorrect. The Directory Setup application is the program for configuring directory services in Mac OS X. Answer b is incorrect. The Console is a Mac OS X application whose primary function is to display the Mac OS X system.log as entries are being written to it. The Console application can also be used to display the contents of other logs such as ftp and NetInfo.

Answer d is incorrect. The Users preference pane is the Mac OS X software where admin and normal user accounts are created and deleted; it is also the location where account passwords can be changed.

Question 15

Answer c is correct. Mac OS 9 legacy applications are referred to as Classic applications. Answer a is incorrect. There is no such thing as Standard applications. Answer b is incorrect. Carbon applications are Mac OS 9 applications that have been modernized to run natively in either Mac OS 9 or OS X. Answer d is incorrect. Packages, sometimes referred to as bundles, are single icon point-and-click representations that correspond with specific applications and can be composed of multiple subordinate files and resources.

Question 16

Answer a is correct. QuickTime is Apple's cross-platform multimedia authoring and distribution engine. Answer b is incorrect. OpenGL is industry standard for three-dimensional (3D) graphics rendering. Answer c is incorrect. Quartz is Apple's moniker for its two-dimensional (2D) graphics-rendering system. Answer d is incorrect. A PDF is a platform agnostic file format that was developed by Adobe to share data electronically.

Question 17

Answer a is correct. In the event that an admin user forgets his or her password, it can be reset from another accessible admin user account.

Question 18

Answer c is correct. The Dock is the Aqua GUI element that can be customized to hold frequently accessed applications. Answer a is incorrect. The Apple Menu in OS X cannot be customized to hold frequently accessed applications. Answer b is incorrect. As shipped, Mac OS X pop-up menus cannot be customized to hold frequently accessed applications. Answer d is incorrect. The Start Menu is a GUI element of Microsoft operating systems.

Question 19

Answer d is correct. In Mac OS X, DHCP is configured in the Network preference pane. Answer a is incorrect. The Network Utility is a set of Mac OS X diagnostic tools for troubleshooting networking issues. Answer b is incorrect. The Internet preference pane is a central location to configure and store preferences for Internet applications. Answer c is incorrect. The Console is a Mac OS X application that has the primary function to display the Mac OS X system.log as entries are being written to it. The Console application can also be used to display the contents of other logs such as ftp and NetInfo.

Question 20

Answer a is correct. The AppleTalk control panel retains functionality in the Classic application environment. See Table 8.1 for a matrix of which OS 9 control panels retain functionality in the Classic application environment.

Question 21

Answers a, b, and d are correct. Preemptive multitasking, protected memory, and symmetric multiprocessing are all considered features of a modern OS. Preemptive multitasking prioritizes processor tasks by order of importance. Protected memory isolates applications in their own individual memory workspaces. In the event of an application crash, the program can be terminated without having a negative effect on other running applications or requiring a restart of the computer. Symmetric multiprocessing provides support for multiprocessor Macintosh computer systems. Answer c is incorrect. Cooperative multitasking is an inefficient way to manage software utilizing of a CPU. As a result, renegade applications can commandeer the system, virtually locking it into one task.

Question 22

Answer e is correct. POP, IMAP, UNIX, and iTools are all supported servers for Mac OS X's Mail application. Answers a, b, c, and d are incorrect as they stand individually, but together they comprise the correct answer of e.

Question 23

Answer b is correct. Additional users for FTP access are added through the Users preference pane. Answer a is incorrect. The Network preference pane is responsible for configuring all networking preferences within Mac OS X. Answer c is incorrect. The Login preference pane can configure options for the Login Window as well as Login Items that will automatically start upon login. Answer d is incorrect. The Internet preference pane is a central location to configure and store preferences for Internet applications.

Question 24

Answer b is correct. The Classic application environment's TCP/IP settings are configured through Mac OS X's Network preference pane. Answer a is incorrect. The Network Utility is a set of Mac OS X diagnostic tools for troubleshooting networking issues. Answer c is incorrect. The Internet preference pane is a central location to configure and store preferences for Internet applications. Answer d is incorrect. Mac OS 9's TCP/IP control panel does not retain functionality in Mac OS X. See Table 8.1 for a matrix of which OS 9 control panels retain functionality in the Classic application environment.

Question 25

Answer b is correct. Symmetric multiprocessing provides support for multiprocessor Macintosh computer systems. Answer a is incorrect. The Classic Application environment allows OS X to run most Macintosh legacy applications that have not been updated to run natively. Answer c is incorrect. Cooperative multitasking is an inefficient way to manage software utilizing of a CPU. As a result, renegade applications can commandeer the system, virtually locking it into one task. Answer d is incorrect. Preemptive multitasking prioritizes processor tasks by order of importance.

Question 26

Answer d is correct. The Mach 3.0 microkernel is the foundation that provides basic services for all other parts of the operating system. It is Mach that gives OS X the features of protected memory architecture, preemptive multitasking, and symmetric multiprocessing. Answer a is incorrect. This is just a bogus statement; Mach is a term used to measure the speed of supersonic aircraft. Answer b is incorrect. Mach is not the term for an OS X native application. Answer c is incorrect. Mach is not a synonym for Mac OS X's command line.

Question 27

Answer a is correct. Mac OS X has built-in support for AppleTalk-based printing, but in order do this the AppleTalk networking protocol must first be enabled within the Network preference pane.

Question 28

Answer d is correct. rw-r--r-- indicates that everyone has Read Privileges, the group has Read Privileges, and the owner has Read & Write Privileges. See Chapter 5 for further review of reading privileges as viewed through the command line. Answers a, b, and c are incorrect as they stand individually, though together they do comprise the correct answer of d.

Question 29

Answer a is correct. The Ping tool, which is a component of the Network Utility, can be used to validate the connectivity of another IP-aware networking device on the Internet. Answer b is incorrect. The Directory Setup application is the program for configuring access to directory services in Mac OS X. Answer c is incorrect. The Console is a Mac OS X application whose primary function is to display the Mac OS X system.log as entries are being written to it. The Console application can also be used to display the contents of other logs such as ftp and NetInfo. Answer d is incorrect. The Apple System Profiler provides a summarized report of installed hardware and software of a given Mac OS X system.

Question 30

Answer b is correct. Aqua is Apple's designation for Mac OS X's new graphical user interface (GUI). Answer a is incorrect. Classic refers to applications that have not been updated to run in Mac OS X. Classic can also refer to the compatibility environment that allows those applications to run in Mac OS X. Answer c is incorrect. Platinum is the term used to refer to Mac OS 9's GUI's appearance. Answer d is incorrect. Luna is the designation for Windows XP's GUI's appearance.

Question 31

Answer a is correct. Open Type is a native font format of Mac OS X.

Question 32

Answer a is correct. It is indeed possible to configure different network protocols, as in the case of AppleTalk and TCP/IP, to share the same network port.

Question 33

Answers a and d are correct. LDAPv2 and NetInfo are the only *natively* supported directory services in Mac OS X. Answers b and c are incorrect. Windows Active Directory and NDS eDirectory are unsupported in Mac OS X, although someday they might be via a third-party software addition.

Question 34

Answer a is correct. The Print Center is used to configure printer connectivity in Mac OS X. Answer b is incorrect. Desktop Printing is an unsupported technology in Mac OS X. Answer c is incorrect. The Chooser can be used to configure printers solely for the Classic application environment. Answer d is incorrect. The Printer Utility is a Mac OS 9 application that is used to configure the hardware options in Apple manufactured printers.

Question 35

Answer d is correct. Classic is an alternative name for the TrueBlueEnvironment. Answer a is incorrect. Carbon is an application that can run in either Mac OS 9 or OS X. When running within OS X, Carbon applications take advantage of most of OS X's modern OS features, including the Aqua interface. In order for Carbon applications to run within Mac OS 9, the CarbonLib library must be present within the Extensions folder inside the Mac OS 9 System Folder. Answer b is incorrect. Java is a Sun Microsystems–developed programming language. It is platform agnostic and allows its applications to run on any platform as long as it contains a cross-compatible Java Virtual Machine. Answer c is incorrect. Cocoa applications are specifically developed for Mac OS X. They are incompatible with older Macintosh operating systems and therefore will not run on Mac OS 9. Cocoa applications take advantage of all of Mac OS X's modern OS features, such as advanced memory management, preemptive multitasking, symmetric multiprocessing, and the full use of the Aqua interface.

Question 36

Answer b is correct. Deleted user accounts files can be transferred only to an admin user or the root account.

Question 37

Answer d is correct. In Mac OS X, the key combination of Command+V is used to start up in verbose mode. Answers a, b, and c are incorrect. None of those key combinations have an affect in Mac OS X.

Question 38

Answer a is correct. LPR printing allows Mac OS X to print using TCP/IP for a network protocol. Answer b is incorrect. AppleTalk has nothing to do with LPR printing. Answer c is incorrect. PPP is an industry standard for the communication of computing devices over dialup POTS (plain old telephone lines) and BRI (Basic Rate Interface) ISDN (Integrated Services Digital Network) lines. It is typically used by ISPs who meter connectivity for billing purposes. Answer d is incorrect. PPPoE is an implementation of PPP over Ethernet.

Question 39

Answer b is correct. The Directory Setup application is the program for configuring access to directory services in Mac OS X. Answer a is incorrect. The Internet preference pane is a central location to configure and store preferences for Internet applications. Answer c is incorrect. The Network Utility is a set of Mac OS X diagnostic tools for troubleshooting networking issues. Answer d is incorrect. The Network preference pane is responsible for configuring all networking preferences within Mac OS X.

Question 40

Answer d is correct. For a printer that is not supported in Mac OS X, Apple recommends saving the document as a PDF and printing from Mac OS 9. Answer a is incorrect. This may well be the course of action; I don't think that upgrading your OS should warrant the purchase of a new printer. Answer b is incorrect. Although this in theory will work, it compromises Mac OS X's marketability by making the admission that it's not ready for prime time and that you might have to rely on other computers as a workaround. Answer c is not necessarily incorrect, but nor is it the best answer.

Question 41

Answer b is correct. Mac OS 9 has no equivalent of a symbolic link.

Question 42

Answer c is correct. A location is a single point of reference for a set of configurations for networking ports and protocols. Answer a is incorrect. A proxy is an intermediary conduit between a user's workstation and the Internet. Answer b is incorrect. Directory services provide a consolidated user list that can be shared among multiple network services or servers for authentication. Directory services do not provide the services themselves but rather describe how they are set up. Answer d is incorrect. For exam purposes, the Setup Assistant is the tool that aids in the configuration of Mac OS X during installation.

Question 43

Answer a is correct. Protected memory isolates applications in their own individual memory workspaces. In the event of an application crash, the program can be terminated without having a negative effect on other running applications or requiring a restart of the computer. Answer b is incorrect. Symmetric multiprocessing provides support for multiprocessor Macintosh computer systems. Answer c is incorrect. Preemptive multitasking prioritizes processor tasks by order of importance. Answer d is incorrect as a result of answer a.

Question 44

Answer d is correct. **top** is the command that displays processor activity within the Terminal. Answer a is incorrect. The **ls** command will display an abbreviated list of all of the contents of the current directory. Answer b is incorrect. The **ls-l** (long list format) command will display a list of the contents of the current directory that will include attributes of item type, permissions, link count, owner, group, size, date and time of last modification, and item name. Answer d is incorrect. The **sudo** (super user do) command allows for the execution of commands as if you were logged-in as the root user account. In fact, it is not necessary to enable the root user account to use the sudo command. Using the sudo command negates the need to log out and log back in as root to run certain commands. In order to use the sudo command, you will need to be an admin user.

Question 45

Answers a and d are correct. Reboot into single-user mode and use **fsck-y** at the command prompt and reboot off the Mac OS X Installer CD and select Repair Disk from the menu bar are both valid ways to repair a hard disk in OS X. The key here is that any disk repair within Mac OS X cannot be executed while booted in normal user mode from the primary hard disk; this is why answers b and c are incorrect.

Question 46

Answer b is correct. Mac OS 9's control panels do not have any effect on Mac OS X system configurations; conversely, Mac OS X System Preferences do have an effect over Mac OS 9 settings within the Classic application environment.

Question 47

Answers a, b, and d are correct. This question is asking the same thing as question 21, but phrased differently. Preemptive multitasking, protected memory, and symmetric multiprocessing are all considered features of a modern OS. Preemptive multitasking prioritizes processor tasks by order of importance. Protected memory isolates applications in their own individual memory workspaces. In the event of an application crash, the program can be terminated without having a negative effect on other running applications or requiring a restart of the computer. Symmetric multiprocessing provides support for multiprocessor Macintosh computer systems. Answer c is incorrect. Cooperative multitasking is an inefficient way to manage software utilizing of a CPU. As a result, renegade applications can commandeer the system, virtually locking it into one task.

Question 48

Answer d is correct. There is no difference between the root account and the superuser account; they are synonymous. Answers a, b, and c are incorrect as result of answer d.

Question 49

Answer a is correct. Invisible items can be listed via the **Go To Folder** command under the Go menu in the Finder.

Question 50

Answer b is correct. The main advantage of the separate partition strategy is that it provides a safety net in the event that the OS X portion becomes damaged. By separating OS 9 and OS X, you can easily erase and reinstall the OS X portion while preserving the OS 9 portion. Answer a is incorrect. A single partition installation is the quickest way to install Mac OS X. Answers c and d are incorrect as a result of answer b being correct.

Question 51

Answer a is correct. OS X does not have any technical limitations that would prevent a Mac OS 9 machine from being a file-sharing AFP client of a Mac OS X machine.

Question 52

Answer b is correct. HFS+ is the preferred format for a Mac OS X volume. This is because HFS+'s single greatest advantage is that it is a "case preserving." format. All Macintosh desktop OSs to date have utilized file systems that have been dependent on case-preserving formatted volumes (this includes the old HFS format as well). Apple ships all OS 9 computers as HFS+; this will provide the most transparent path for file migration to OS X. Answer a is incorrect. A UFS-formatted disk has technical limitations in Mac OS X, none the least being that it is case sensitive. AirPort is incompatible and inaccessible from Mac OS 9, and special attention (extra effort) is needed in order to run Classic from a UFS-formatted volume. Answer c is incorrect. NFS (Network File System) is the Unix equivalent of personal file sharing. It allows users to view and store files on a remote computer. Answer d is incorrect. HFS, sometimes referred to as Standard format, was Apple's original hard disk format for the Macintosh. Approximately sometime in 1998 Apple dumped it in favor of HFS+ format (Extended Format). HFS+ was designed to address capacity and all-around technical limitations that prevented HFS as a suitable format for modern-day computing.

Question 53

Answer a is correct. Darwin is an Open Source community/Apple joint effort. The primary objective of the Darwin project is to build an industrial-strength UNIX-based operating system core that would provide greater stability and performance compared to the existing iterations of the Mac OS to date. Answer b is incorrect. QuickTime is Apple's name for its cross-platform multimedia authoring and distribution platform. Answer c is incorrect. While this might be true, it has no application in reference to Mac OS X. Answer d is incorrect. Open GL is a standard graphics Application Programming Interface (API) by which software and hardware manufacturers can build 3D applications and hardware across multiple platforms on a common standard.

Question 54

Answer c is correct. The **man** (manual pages) command provides an online collection of reference manuals pages detailing just about every command that can be executed from the command prompt within Mac OS X. Answer a is incorrect. The **chmod** (change mode) command offers similar functionality to the Privileges portion of the Show Info command from within the Finder. It can be used to change the definition of access privileges for a file or set of files. Answer b is incorrect. The **ls** command will display an abbreviated list of all of the contents of the current directory. Answer d is incorrect. The **chown** command can be used to change ownership for a file or set of files.

Question 55

Answer b is correct. The Startup Manager is not a valid way to pick among multiple OS installations on the same partition.

Question 56

Answers d and e are correct. Apple recommends the use of a non-flash camera to take a photograph of the screen. If a camera is unavailable, it is recommended to copy down the information by hand. Answer a is incorrect. The grab application will not function during the event of a kernel panic. Answer b is incorrect. Verbose mode is used to display all system activity during startup in text format. Answer c is incorrect. Due to the nature of a kernel panic, printing is not an available option.

Question 57

Answer a is correct. It is possible to have multiple installations of Mac OS 9 on the same partition as Mac OS X.

Question 58

Answer a is correct. Mac OS X is Apple's first true multiuser operating system.

Question 59

Answer a is correct. AppleTalk and TCP/IP are examples of protocols. A protocol is a set of rules for the exchange of data between computer systems. Answer b is incorrect. A *port*, as referred to within the Network preference pane, is some form of physical connection to a data network. Answer c is incorrect. A proxy is an intermediary conduit between a user's workstation and the Internet. Answer d is incorrect. A topology is a description of a physical arrangement or layout of networking hardware.

Question 60

Answer b is correct. A UFS-formatted partition does not support AirPort connectivity in Mac OS X. Answer a is incorrect. UFS formatting supports Classic albeit with some extra effort as described in Apple Knowledge Base Article ID 106277, entitled: Mac OS X 10.0: Classic Does Not Work From a UFS Disk on First Use. Answer c is incorrect. UFS is a case-sensitive format. Answer d is incorrect. Mac OS X does support UFS-formatted partitions.

Question 61

Answer b is correct. It is not possible to kill processes that are not owned by the user from within the ProcessViewer application.

Question 62

Answer a is correct. Login Items are the functional equivalent of Mac OS 9's Startup Items. Answer b is incorrect. A pane is an Aqua GUI element composed of separate screens within a window that is typically accessed via a pop-up menu or tab. Panes redraw themselves within the confines of the initial window. Answer c is incorrect. A Sheet is an Aqua GUI element composed of a dialog box the draws (emanates) itself out of an active file window. Answer d is incorrect. System preferences are Mac OS X's equivalent of Mac OS 9's control panels.

Question 63

Answer b is correct. Within Mac OS X, the maximum number of groups that can be assigned an item is one. Answers b, c, d are incorrect as a result of answer a.

Question 64

Answer a is correct. In Mac OS X, it is possible to configure language preferences for a specific application on an application-by-application basis.

Question 65

Answer b is correct. A search path is a hierarchically ordered acquisition of system resources. Answer a is incorrect. DNS (Domain Name System) is a service that resolves domain names to IP addresses and vice versa. Answer c is incorrect. A file system is a method of organizing data on storage media. Answer d is incorrect. Privileges provide the control mechanism for user access to files, folders, and applications within Mac OS X.

Question 66

Answer b is correct. The Disk Utility is the program that formats and partitions hard disks in Mac OS X. Answer a is incorrect. Drive Setup is Mac OS 9's program that formats and partitions hard disks. Answer c is incorrect. Disk First Aid is Mac OS 9's program that is used to verify and repair the data structure of hard disks. Answer d is incorrect. The Directory Setup application is the program for configuring access to directory services in Mac OS X.

Question 67

Answers b and d are correct. The / Library/Fonts and the Mac OS 9 Fonts folders are the only two directories within Mac OS X that can store fonts that can be accessed globally throughout the entire system. Answer a is incorrect. The ~/ Library/Fonts folder are fonts that can be accessed only by the specific user of that home directory. Answer c is incorrect. The /System/Library/Fonts folder, which is the Fonts folder inside the Library folder inside the System folder, contains the default fonts required by the operating system and must not be altered.

Question 68

Answer a is correct. The ~ (tilde) represents a user's Home folder within the command line. Answers b, c, d are incorrect. System, Fonts, and Applications would be represented by their respective given names within the command line.

Question 69

Answer c is correct. Shared libraries are Mac OS 9's equivalent of Mac OS X's frameworks. Answer a is incorrect. A CDEV (Control Panel Device) would be Mac OS 9's equivalent of Mac OS X's preference panes. Answer b is incorrect. Although not reviewed in the text of this book, Open Transport is Mac OS 9's designation for its underlying networking technology. There is no equivalent of it in Mac OS X. Mac OS X uses an entirely different technology, referred to as *Network Sockets*. Answer d is incorrect as a result of answer c.

Question 70

Answer d is correct. Quartz is a powerful two-dimensional (2D) graphics-rendering system. It has built-in support for the Portable Document Format (PDF), on-the-fly rendering, compositing, and antialiasing. It supports multiple font formats, including TrueType, Postscript Type 1, and OpenType. Quartz supports Apple's ColorSync color-management technology, allowing for consistent and accurate color in the print/graphics environment. Answer a is incorrect. QuickTime is Apple's proprietary cross-platform multimedia authoring and distribution engine. QuickTime is both a file format and a suite of applications. Answer b is incorrect. OpenGL is an industry standard for three-dimensional (3D) graphics rendering. It provides a standard graphics Application Programming Interface (API) by which software and hardware manufacturers can build 3D applications and hardware across multiple platforms on a common standard. Answer c is incorrect. QuickDraw is a Mac OS 9 graphics-rendering technology.

Question 71

Answers b, c, and d are correct. By force-quitting the process through the ProcessViewer application, or by using the Force Quit command located under the Apple Menu, or by using the key combination Option+Command+Esc, it is possible to force quit an unresponsive application in Mac OS X. Option+Command+Esc is the keyboard command equivalent of the **Force Quit** command located under the Apple Menu. Answer a is incorrect because **top** is the command that displays processor activity within the Terminal.

Question 72

Answer a is correct. Public is the name of the folder that users can place their files into, in order to share them over a network. Answer b is incorrect. The Users folder is the parent directory for all Home folders for local user accounts. Answer c is incorrect. The Shared folder is the place where local user accounts can share files among themselves locally on the system. Answer d is incorrect. The Drop Box folder provides a safe haven for remotely connected users to place contents on the machine in a secure manner without the prying eyes of other connected users.

Question 73

Answers a, b, c, and d are all correct. Login Items, new user accounts, passwords, and Disable Restart and Shut Down buttons are all options that cannot be configured from the login window. User accounts and passwords are configured through the Users preference pane, and the Disable Restart and Shut Down buttons are configured through the Login preference pane.

Question 74

Answers b, c, and d are correct. The command line can be accessed using >console, Terminal and Remote SSH. Answer a is incorrect. Verbose mode is used to display all system activity during startup in text format.

Question 75

Answer b is correct. DeskTop printing is an unsupported technology in Mac OS X.

Question 76

Answer b is correct. PPPoE cannot be configured for an analog modem. PPPoE is an implementation of PPP over Ethernet and thus can only be utilized with Ethernet devices.

Question 77

Answer c is correct. OS 9.1 is the minimum version of Mac OS 9 that can be used with the Classic application environment.

Question 78

Answer b is correct. Mac OS X does not require a system restart after an external USB hard disk is plugged in.

Question 79

Answer c is correct. User accounts are administered through the Users preference pane. Answer a is incorrect. File sharing, Web sharing and ftp access are administered through the Sharing preference pane. Answer b is incorrect. Login items and Login Window preferences are administered through the Login preference pane. Answer d is incorrect. Network settings and configurations are administered through the Network preference pane.

Question 80

Answer b is correct. Network printing will not function when the BSD subsystem is not selected as part of a Mac OS X installation. Answers a and c are incorrect because they have no bearing on the inclusion of the BSD subsystem. Answer d is incorrect as a result of answer b.

Glossary

admin

An account that has access to all of Mac OS X's system preferences and utilities and provides the ability to install applications and system-wide resources. An admin account also provides the ability to create and manage other user accounts and enable the root account, if needed, within an OS X system.

adopted ownership

The transfer of ownership of the contents of a deleted user's home folder to an administrator's user account.

advanced memory management

Automatically manages physical RAM and virtual memory dynamically as needed.

AirPort

Apple's brand moniker for its wireless networking product line.

alias

A representative file that can dynamically locate its target file or folder, even if you move that file or folder to a different location within the same volume.

Apache

An Open Source licensed Web server that is the Web-serving engine of Mac OS X.

AppleCare Knowledge Base

The official Apple Web-based technical library for the support of its products.

Apple Menu

The menu displayed when the apple-shaped icon in the upper-left corner of the menu bar is clicked on.

AppleScript

An Apple proprietary technology that is a scripting language allowing for the automation of Mac OS–based computing tasks.

AppleTalk
A proprietary networking protocol created by Apple Computer.

API (Application Programming Interface)
A set of programming calls used by application developers to access routines in other applications and operating system components.

Applications folder
The Applications folder contains all user-accessible software programs. These programs can include productivity applications, games, and utilities (which have their own subfolders).

Aqua
Apple's designation for Mac OS X's new graphical user interface (GUI).

architecture
The logical design of a system.

authoritative DNS server
A DNS server that can hold the DNS entries for IP-aware entities connected to the Internet. See also DNS (Domain Name Service).

backup
The program used to protect against data loss as a result of data corruption, hardware failures, viruses, and (if operated offsite) natural disasters and theft.

boot
To start a computer and load its operating system.

BSD (Berkeley Software Distribution)
A particular version of Unix that was developed at and distributed from the University of California at Berkeley. It is the flavor of Unix on which Mac OS X is based.

BSD Subsystem
A required component of an Mac OS X installation that is necessary for proper network functionality and network printing.

bundle
See *package*.

Carbon
A type of application that can run in either Mac OS 9 or Mac OS X. When running within OS X, Carbon applications take advantage of most of OS X's modern OS features, including the Aqua interface. In order for Carbon applications to run within Mac OS 9, the CarbonLib library must be present within the Extensions folder inside the Mac OS 9 System Folder.

Classic
Provides Mac OS X with the ability to run a full version of Mac OS 9 in a protected memory space. This compatibility environment allows the user to run most Macintosh legacy software that has not been updated to run natively in OS X.

Cocoa
Applications that are specifically developed for Mac OS X. Cocoa applications are incompatible with older Macintosh operating systems and therefore will not run on Mac OS 9. Cocoa applications take advantage of all of Mac OS X's modern features, such as advanced memory management, preemptive multitasking, symmetric multiprocessing, and the Aqua interface.

command-line interface
Provides a non-GUI way of interacting with Mac OS X via text commands.

Darwin
A project that's a joint effort between the Open Source community and Apple. The primary objective of the Darwin project is to build an industrial-strength Unix-based operating system core that provides greater stability and performance compared to the existing iterations of the Mac OS to date.

device
A piece of hardware attached to a computer that is capable of providing input or output or both.

DHCP (Dynamic Host Configuration)
A networking service that dynamically assigns TCP/IP addresses to client computers.

dialog box
A GUI element that allows the user to interact with the computer.

directory
Another term for a folder.

Directory Services
Directory Services provide a consolidated user list that can be shared among multiple network services or servers for authentication. Directory Services do not provide the services themselves but rather describe how they are set up.

DNS (Domain Name System)
A service that resolves domain names to IP addresses, and vice versa.

driver
A piece of software that enables an operating system to control a hardware device.

Drop Box
A folder located inside a user's public folder that allows other users to "drop off" files via the network when peer-to-peer file sharing is enabled.

dual-boot capability
Allows a computer to boot from multiple operating systems. The user has the ability to select which operating system will run at startup.

file extension
A designation included in the name of a file in order to help associate it with its appropriate parent application.

file sharing
See *peer-to-peer file sharing*.

file system
It is a method of organizing data on storage media.

Finder
The application that allows users to graphically interact with the contents of both their computer and network servers.

firmware
Low-level programming that tells a computer's hardware how to behave.

frameworks
Mac OS X frameworks are analogous to Mac OS 9 shared libraries in that they both contain dynamically loading code that is shared by multiple applications. Frameworks alleviate the need for applications that

contain common code to load that code multiple times when running simultaneously.

FTP (File Transfer Protocol)
Provides a means of moving files between computers over a TCP/IP network.

group
Used to simplify the assignment of system access to a series of users intended to share the same level of system access.

GUI (Graphical User Interface)
Provides a graphical way of interacting with Mac OS X via point-and-click visual elements.

HFS+ (Hierarchical File System Plus)
An extended file format designed for high-capacity hard drives that is case preserving and supports file names greater than 31 characters.

home folder
The folder in which a user stores all personal files within a Mac OS X system.

iDisk
A service within iTools that provides an Internet-accessible storage space for data.

inherited permissions
Privileges that propagate from a parent folder to child folders and files.

IP address
A unique 32-bit binary number that is used to represent a computer on the Internet.

iTools
A free set of Internet-based services that includes, but is not limited to, email, Web serving, and data storage. These are available to all Mac users at no charge.

Java
A programming language developed by Sun Microsystems. Java is platform agnostic, allowing its applications to run on any platform as long as it contains a cross-compatible Java Virtual Machine.

kernel/microkernel
The foundation that provides basic services for all other parts of the operating system. See *Mach 3.0 microkernel*.

LDAP (Lightweight Directory Access Protocol)
A software protocol that enables the location of individuals, organizations, and other resources such as files and devices on a network.

Library folder
Library folders that are located in a user's home directory contain user-customizable resources and preferences for Mac OS X.

localhost
A generic name of a machine linked to an IP address.

LocalTalk
An Apple proprietary networking topology that is unsupported in Mac OS X.

log in
To identify yourself as a particular user by entering a name and password

at the login window in order to gain access to your user account.

log out
A command to quit current user settings and return the OS X system back to the login screen.

LPR (Line Print Remote) printer
A printer that contains a protocol that allows it to print via TCP/IP.

Mach 3.0 microkernel
Developed at Carnegie-Mellon University, the Mach 3.0 microkernel has a closely tied history with BSD (Berkeley Software Distribution) Unix. Mach gives OS X the features of protected memory architecture, preemptive multitasking, and symmetric multiprocessing.

modem
A device that allows a computer or other digital device to use an analog or digital telephone line to communicate with other computers or digital devices.

NetInfo
The native directory service for Mac OS X. A NetInfo database/directory is referred to as a *domain*. The NetInfo database is hierarchical and contains both local and network user as well as group authentication information.

NFS (Network File System)
The Unix equivalent of personal file sharing. NFS allows users to view and store files on a remote computer.

OpenGL (Open Graphics Library)
An industry standard for three-dimensional (3D) graphics rendering.

It provides a standard graphics application programming interface (API) by which software and hardware manufacturers can build 3D applications and hardware across multiple platforms on a common standard.

Open Source software
Typically, software developed as a public collaboration and made freely available.

OS (operating system)
The software that acts as the intermediary (the glue) between the user, the computer, the peripheral devices, and the applications.

package
Sometimes referred to as a *bundle*, a package is a single icon point-and-click representation of an application. Just like previous Classic applications, Mac OS X's Carbon and Cocoa applications can be composed of multiple subordinate files and resources. In the GUI, all these subordinate pieces are neatly wrapped up into a representation of a single executable file for the end user.

pane
An Aqua GUI element composed of separate screens within a window that is typically accessed via a pop-up menu or tab. Panes redraw themselves within the confines of the initial window.

partition
An identifiable logical division of a hard disk.

path
The route to a specific file. A pathname is the map of that path.

PDF (Portable Document Format)

A platform-agnostic file format developed by Adobe to share data electronically. PDF files are typically used in lieu of physically printed documents.

peer-to-peer file sharing

A decentralized system of sharing and transferring files between users without using a server.

peripheral

See *device.*

permissions

See *privileges.*

ping

A support tool that can be used to validate the connectivity of another IP-aware networking device on the Internet.

POP (Post Office Protocol)

A client/server store-and-forward protocol for the receipt of email.

port

As referred to within the Network preference pane, a port is some form of physical connection to a data network.

Postscript printer

A printer that supports an Adobe-developed industry standard for a mathematical programming language that electronically describes the appearance of printed material. It is utilized in print/graphics environments where precise and accurate printing is a must.

PPoE (Point-to-Point Protocol over Ethernet)

An implementation of PPP over Ethernet, and is typically used by ISPs that want to regulate access or meter usage of its subscribers.

PPP (Point-to-Point Protocol)

An industry standard for the communication of computing devices over dial-up POTS (plain-old telephone lines) and BRI (Basic Rate Interface) ISDN (Integrated Services Digital Network) lines.

PRAM (parameter RAM or parameter random-access memory)

A battery-powered form of random-access memory where system information, such as the date and time, is stored.

preemptive multitasking

Prioritizes processor tasks by order of importance. Preemptive multitasking allows the computer to handle multiple tasks simultaneously. This method of managing processor tasks more efficiently allows the computer to remain responsive, even during the most processor-intensive tasks.

privileges

Provide the control mechanism for user access to files, folders, and applications within Mac OS X.

process

Can be either an entire program or threads (tasks) within a program.

protected memory

Isolates applications in their individual memory workspaces. In the event of an application crash, the program can be terminated without having a negative effect on other running applications or requiring a restart of the computer.

protocol

A set of rules for the exchange of data between computer systems.

proxy

Typically employs a server that acts as an intermediary between a user's workstation and the Internet. When a request is made for Internet content, the request is passed along to the proxy server. The proxy server acts on behalf of the client and forwards the request on to the Internet. It then relates the retrieved response back to the user.

Quartz

A powerful two-dimensional (2D) graphics-rendering system. Quartz has built-in support for the Portable Document Format (PDF), on-the-fly rendering, compositing, and antialiasing. It supports multiple font formats, including TrueType, Post-script Type 1, and OpenType. Quartz supports Apple's ColorSync color-management technology, allowing for consistent and accurate color in the print/graphics environment.

QuickTime

Apple's proprietary cross-platform multimedia authoring and distribution engine. QuickTime is both a file format and a suite of applications.

root

Sometimes referred to as the *system administrator* or the *superuser account*,

root has complete access to all settings and files within the operating system. Root is also used as a term that refers to the top-level directory of a file system.

search path

An ordered search for resources within a Mac OS X system.

Shared Folder

The place where local user accounts can share files among themselves locally on the system.

sheet

An Aqua GUI element composed of a dialog box that draws (emanates) itself out of an active file window.

single-user mode

Entered during system startup by holding down Command+S at boot time. Single-user mode circumvents the GUI for the command line. A feature of single-user mode is that it disables multiuser processes. It's typically used for troubleshooting purposes.

SMTP (Simple Mail Transfer Protocol)

A protocol typically used in sending email from an email client, although it is also used for sending and receiving email between email servers.

SSH (Secure Shell)

A protocol for securely accessing a remote computer.

subnet mask

A 32-bit binary number that is used to identify a segment of a network.

symbolic link

A representative file that contains exact information (hard encoded) as to where a file or folder resides.

symmetric multiprocessing

The technology that allows developers to build applications that take advantage of two or more processors by assigning applications to a specific processor or by splitting an application's tasks between multiple processors simultaneously.

TCP/IP (Transmission Control Protocol/Internet Protocol)

The basic communication language of the Internet.

Telnet

An application that allows *remote* users to interact with Mac OS X's command line over TCP/IP, assuming they have been given permission.

Terminal

An application that allows users to interact with Mac OS X's command line.

topology

A description of a physical arrangement or layout of networking hardware.

TrueType

A scalable font technology created by Apple.

UFS (Unix File System)

A nonpreferred file system format for OS X. UFS does not support AirPort networking and is case sensitive. In addition, UFS volumes do not show up when booted from Mac OS 9, their volume names cannot be customized, and special attention (in other words, extra effort) is needed in order to run Classic from a UFS volume.

user

A non-techie whose existence is a techie's job security. A normal user account does not allow for system-wide administration of Mac OS X.

user preferences

Unique settings that users configure for applications and system software.

verbose mode

Displays all system activity in text format during the boot process.

volume

See *partition*.

Index